Why Did
I Buy This
Book?

Why Did I Buy This Book?

Over 500 Puzzlers, Teasers, and Challenges

to Boost Your **BRAINPOWER**

by Lynn Brunelle

CHRONICLE BOOKS
SAN FRANCISCO

Library of Congress Cataloging-in-Publication Data
Brunelle, Lynn.
    Why did I buy this book? : over 500 puzzlers, teasers, and
challenges to boost your brainpower / by Lynn Brunelle.
        p. cm.
    ISBN 978-0-8118-6686-6
    1. Puzzles. I. Title
GV1493.B697 2009
793.73—dc22

                                                2008038467

Manufactured in Canada
Designed by Jennifer Tolo Pierce
Typesetting by Janis Reed
Illustrations by Lynn Brunelle

10 9 8 7 6 5 4 3 2 1

Chronicle Books LLC
680 Second Street
San Francisco, CA 94107

www.chroniclebooks.com

For all the forgetters I'll never forget.

TABLE OF CONTENTS

Foreword

By Ira Flatow
Host of *Science Friday*

Decades before all the current research about the brain and memory, my dad, Sam, said that if you wanted to stay sharp you needed to "exercise" your brain. He drilled that message into me countless times. What he didn't know is why the brain can be helped by exercise. Today, we know better.

Our brains are made of a hundred billion nerve cells. Each of these nerve cells is networked to tens of thousands of others. We used to think that the neurons we were born with were all the brain cells we were ever going to get. So, if the neurons were damaged by stroke or trauma to the head, you would never be able to regain the functions they served, such as speaking or walking.

Today, we know that's not true. We know that our brain is very plastic and pliable; it has the ability to regain functions it might have lost. People whose speech is impaired by stroke lose some functioning in their arms or legs, but are able to regain those functions from exercise. Healthy parts of a damaged brain are even able to help take over functions of the damaged part. And most importantly, we know that the brain can grow new nerve cells. Stem cells are able to grow into functioning neurons.

What all this means is that the brain can rewire itself for learning and memory, too. Experiments with laboratory animals show that when they learn a new task, they strengthen the synapses—the connections between the brain cells. And now, with the exercises in this book, you'll be able to remember why you bought it in the first place.

Introduction

Admit it.

It's happened to you.

You park the car and you can't remember where the heck you left it. You lose your keys for the *umpteenth* time. That guy in accounting always says "Hi" and you have *no idea* what his name is—even though you have been introduced a half dozen times. Your daughter tells a funny story about how you were covered with cake on her tenth birthday party. Obviously you were there, but what the *heck* is she talking about?

It happens to the best of us. It's called getting older—a process that starts as soon as we emerge into the world. But those fuzzy little moments of not feeling like the sharp tack we used to is something that starts to bug us when we reach, oh, a certain age.

Movie titles, book characters, historical events, simple math: All these things seem stowed somewhere ultrasecret or completely erased from your hard drive.

But not to worry. Help is here!

If you've ever had a brainblank (and who hasn't), *Why Did I Buy This Book? Over 500 Puzzlers, Teasers, and Challenges to Boost Your Brainpower* has your name written all over it.

The latest neuroscience research shows that the idea of "use it or lose it" is exactly the ticket when it comes to keeping your brain sharp. Makes sense when you think about it. If you eat donuts and watch TV all day, chances are you are more than a mere shadow of your former physical self. You have to eat right and exercise your body to remain fit, right? Same with your brain. You gotta give your wits a workout.

Puzzles are terrific ways to keep those mental muscles moving and cerebral sparks flying. They spruce up your abilities to reason, analyze, sequence, deduce, think logically, and problem-solve.

This isn't your mom's sudoku. It's a compilation of word games, visual spatial challenges, bad puns, trips down memory lane, logic puzzlers, and memory boosters. With several levels of difficulties and themes, your hard drive will be cleaned up and spinning right along before you know it.

So why did you buy this book? Dive on in, flip through, find a challenge that looks like fun and take it. It won't be long before you remember exactly why.

Chapter One:

WHAT WAS THAT WORD AGAIN?

You don't have to be an aging English major to have fun and benefit from these puzzles. Wordplay and vocabulary games are terrific ways to stimulate your brain and make connections—keeping it supple and fit.

Language itself is one of the first complex journeys our brains take when we're born. From the get-go our brains absorb and process the construction of language. So it makes a lot of sense that exercising these skills is a great way to keep your brain sharp. These puzzles will challenge you to think about complex ideas and word associations and will keep your brain busy maintaining old pathways and creating a few new ones along the way.

See if those crossword puzzles, games of Scrabble, and constant book-reading did the trick for your powers of definition. Get your pun-maker in gear and sort out the homophones. And tap into your inner Seuss-Frost-Eliot-Dickinson-Angelou and try your rhyming skills in Hink-Pinks.

Words—Definitions

Are these words familiar to you? If you don't know them on sight, try to figure out what they mean based on word root.

✳ answers on page 319

1. **GOUACHE**
   A. an Eastern European stew
   B. a method of painting
   C. a medical term for false pain

   _____

2. **BIVALVE**
   A. a mollusk in a hinged shell
   B. a hot and cold water faucet
   C. a cow's heart

   _____

3. PILOT
   A. the final episode in a TV series
   B. an electric switch
   C. a ship's helmsman

_____

4. BILGE
   A. discarded, rotting produce
   B. an offensive burp
   C. the rounded-out part of a barrel

_____

5. PLANTAIN
   A. the farmland at a mountain's base
   B. a type of banana
   C. a glass-enclosed porch

_____

6. WORSTED

    A. a smooth, long-fibered yarn

    B. the opposite of bested

    C. a heavy application of eye makeup

---

7. SYLLABUS

    A. a British dessert

    B. the outline of an academic course

    C. an old-fashioned joke book

8. **PORTENT**
   A. a glass for serving liqueur
   B. turning a ship or plane leftward
   C. an omen of things to come

   _____

9. **FEBRILE**
   A. feverish
   B. a species of houseplant
   C. easily broken

   _____

10. VERISIMILITUDE

    A. a talent for defining words

    B. the quality of appearing real

    C. a description of fraternal twins

    _____

11. POPINJAY

    A. a supercilious person

    B. a rubber duck

    C. a form of breakfast muffin

    _____

12. BELLICOSE

    A. "beautiful cousin" in Italian

    B. a little white lie

    C. inclined to provoke quarrels

    _____

13. OBSEQUIOUS
  A. out of chronological order
  B. a fawning, subservient manner
  C. entertaining, hilarious

_____

14. PANTHEISM
  A. the study of the planets
  B. the classic guide to trouser design
  C. the belief in numerous gods

_____

15. ACTUARY
  A. a calculator of statistical probabilities
  B. the setting for improvisational theater
  C. an area within a cathedral

_____

16. **INTERSTICE**

   A. the space between things

   B. an especially fancy sewing method

   C. a conversation-stopping remark

   _____

17. **CRINOLINE**

   A. literally, a crinkly line

   B. a stiff cotton or horsehair fabric

   C. a type of hairless poodle

   _____

18. GARRULOUS

    A. excessively talkative

    B. red-faced

    C. given to constant throat-clearing

_____

19. ALPACA

    A. a Native American infant's sling

    B. a woolly Peruvian animal

    C. an ancient copper coin

_____

20. UNGAINLY

    A. given to losing weight

    B. sluggish stocks and bonds

    C. clumsy

_____

21. TABULAR

A. having a flat surface
B. a form of newspaper
C. catlike

22. PEDANTIC

A. two-footed, nonhuman animals
B. narrow, often showy studiousness
C. a comical walking style

23. LEGUME

A. an Apache symbol of power
B. a French salad fork
C. a peapod

24. PERNICIOUS

  A. funny

  B. destructive

  C. irritating

---

25. ALLOY

  A. a combination of metals

  B. Benjamin Franklin's middle name

  C. a naval greeting

Hink-Pinks, or Rhyming Pairs

Creating rhyming pairs develops phonological awareness. When you make words that sound alike, you're using the areas of your brain that focus on language and sound, as well as making connections between concepts. Can you find the rhyming pairs based on these clues? Hink-Pinks have one syllable in each word, Hinky-Pinkys have two, and Hinkity-Pinkitys have three.

* answers on page 320

1. What is this Hink-Pink for a lackluster crustacean?

_____

_____

2. What is this Hinky-Pinky for a crustacean modeled after Tony Soprano?

_____

_____

3. What is this Hinky-Pinky for a fowl practicing witchcraft?

_____

_____

4. Name this Hink-Pink for a young man fond of pounded taro-root paste.

_____

_____

5. What is this Hink-Pink for a housekeeping employee who enjoys being out of direct sunlight?

_____

_____

6. Name this Hinkity-Pinkity for an infant swaddled in designer wool clothing.

_____

_____

7. What is this Hink-Pink for a contest where the greatest "pertusser" reigns?

_____

_____

8. Name this Hink-Pink for a vehicle carrying an urban pest.

_____

_____

9. What is this Hinky-Pinky for a shelled reptile with bountiful offspring?

_____

_____

10. What's this Hink-Pink for a recording device concentrating on what fashionable folks wear?

_____

_____

11. What's a Hinky-Pinky for a mother who's gone tropical?

_____

_____

12. What's a Hinky-Pinky for a person who enjoys setting flame to paper art images made for hanging on walls?

_____

_____

13. What's a Hink-Pink for a musical group that gets fired from their gig?

_____

_____

14. If Kermit used frog polish he'd have this Hink-Pink.

_____

_____

15. What Hinky-Pinky describes a mama wolf's snout rubbing against her baby?

_____

_____

16. Name the Hink-Pink you get when you first try to make a call.

_____

_____

17. What's a Hink-Pink for a happy father?

_____

_____

18. This Hinky-Pinky describes the gossip you might hear when you take the dog in for a bath.

_____

_____

19. What's a Hinky-Pinky for a big, dozy conical tent?

_____

_____

20. This Hinky-Pinky is a suspicious female.

_____

_____

21. A knife can be this Hinky-Pinky—especially
at toast time.

_____

_____

22. Intelligent creative works are this Hink-Pink.

_____

_____

23. A dog with technique and a twig is all you need for this Hink-Pink.

_____

_____

24. This Hink-Pink is a free fowl!

_____

_____

25. A chanteuse and a stand-up comedienne, this Hinky-Pinky is both.

_____

_____

Homophones

Homophones are pairs of words that sound the same but are spelled differently and have different meanings. In these puzzles, the homophones have been removed. Can you figure out what the real words should be?

✳ answers on page 321

For example:

Sal didn't know he had to pay sales _____ on a box of _____.

Tax/tacks

1.   After the _____ in the paper, Randy could hardly _____ up the orders fast enough!

2.   Keith thought everyone knew that the solution for anything that might _____ was a frosty glass of _____.

3. Leo used a paste made from _____ and water to make a _____ for his mother that would never wilt.

4. The village _____ was an adept chef, and people came from miles around to see what he had cooking in his _____.

5. Ella felt that every _____ on her face was so big, she could _____ an entire glass of water into each.

6. Sean used _____ to figure out how many slices of _____ to serve to the family.

7. The grandkids were the picture of _____ and happiness until the last _____ of pizza was up for grabs.

8. _____ the holes Ayla made in the leather garment were made with her trusty _____.

9. Edna suspected that if she dressed in plastic _____ and gyrated to some _____ music, she might work Edgar into an amorous state.

10. Felicity's new _____ was pleased when she wore a _____ in her hair.

11. Chip wasn't sure what _____ the dinner _____ played—soup sopper or between-courses palate cleanser?

12. Samantha found a small _____ in her new _____ hat.

13. Dizzy _____ his trumpet until he was _____ in the face.

14. All _____ the _____ and hearty!

15. You didn't _____ this from me, but do you know who was _____ this afternoon?

16. During the test, Kai knew that it was important to write _____ answer in the blank, but he wanted to make sure he figured the _____ correctly in the first place.

17. Sheena had to offer a _____ salary in order to _____ the candidate she wanted.

18. Abigail had no idea that the charming _____ ride would end in her desire to _____ the driver.

19. Alex ate a _____ as he listened to the throbbing _____ of Rosie's new song.

20. When Lisa lost her _____ down the drain, she couldn't help but _____ her hands in worry.

21. Everyone _____ that a _____ smells!

22. Lynn took the afternoon to wander the _____ and was struck with how many _____ items there were.

23. Jim didn't even set foot _____ the _____ because he didn't like the look of it.

24. Bill _____ his bed every morning, even on days that the _____ was coming.

25. Keith began to _____ when he saw how his lawn had not been _____ for a month.

Memory Box #1

Where did that file go? What time is my meeting? Short-term memory taking a little snooze on the job? Perk it up with this memory puzzle.

Take a close look at the images on this page. Give yourself a minute. Then, turn the page and see how many questions you can answer.

* answers on page 322

1. How many computers were there?

   _____

2. What day is it?

   _____

3. Is the founder male or female?

   _____

4. How many coffee cups were there?

   _____

5. How many had only one stripe?

   _____

6. Was the cooler half full or a quarter empty?

   _____

7. In what city is this office found?

_____

8. Could the phone have been ringing?

_____

9. Were all-time high sales in February or April?

_____

10. How many potted plants are there?

_____

Chapter Two:

WHO WAS THAT?

Plunge into this mixed bag of pop culture and history trivia questions and take a little trip (don't fall!) down memory lane.

Music, visual cues, and story recall are great ways to stimulate the cerebral cortex. It's all about making connections. Over the years your brain makes shortcuts allowing you to multitask and be more efficient. In the long run, though, you want to override those shortcuts and create new pathways. Trivia and content challenges are a great way to perk up pathways. Recalling subjects like books, movies, and music can create new pathways and get you sizzling cerebrally!

So get a little brain blast from the past. Name those tunes, discover some fun film facts, and test your book IQ, literally.

Sing It!

We know the songs, we love the words, but what's the name of that song? Dig deep into your memory vault and try your hand, and ear, at these musical questions.

✳ answers on pages 322–324

1. Name Paul Simon's song about extraction.

_____

2. What ecosystem did America get through? And how did they travel?

_____

3. Where was the Monkees' final train headed?

_____

4. Name Simon and Garfunkel's song about the power of listening.

_____

5. Name these three B-52's songs: the one about the crustacean, the one about the northwestern state, and the one about the amorous construction.

_____

_____

6. What is Joni Mitchell's geometric pastime?

_____

7. Name these two songs by David Byrne's band— the one about an inferno and the one that you might want right afterward.

_____

_____

8. Bill Clinton and Al Gore used this Fleetwood Mac song for a campaign message.

_____

9. Name Peter Gabriel's shocking song about primates.

_____

10. What are these three James Taylor songs? The one about a part of a building, the one about a guy moving along on foot, and the one about a construction vehicle.

_____

_____

_____

11. Name Elvis's two "blue" songs.

_____

_____

12. What color do the Rolling Stones want to
    paint things?

_____

13. What does BTO stand for and what do they
    think you've seen?

    _____

    _____

14. Who's got a mohair suit and electric boots?
    What song is she in and who sang it?

    _____

    _____

15. What is Led Zeppelin's famous passage up?

    _____

16. What is Lynryd Skynyrd's blue-skied home-
    sweet-home song?

    _____

17. What is Tom Jones's famous feline inquiry?

    _____

18. Who sang the "Monster Mash"?

_____

19. What was Dusty Springfield's song about a
relative of a man of the cloth?

_____

20. Name the three Police guys and then name
their first hit.

_____

_____

_____

_____

21. What was MTV's very first video?

_____

22. Who sang backup on Carly Simon's hit "You're So Vain"?

_____

23. What do the letters in ABBA stand for?

_____

_____

_____

_____

24. What kind of weather did Seals and Crofts sing about?

_____

25. Who was "Reelin' in the Years" in 1972?

_____

I Think I Saw This One Already: Film Trivia

These questions are all based on the silver screen. Remember when you saw these stars and their pictures? Who were you with and where did you see them? Test your knowledge of movie trivia.

✳ **answers on pages 324–327**

I. Which of the following lines was **NOT** from *Casablanca*?

"Here's looking at you, kid."

"One thing I can't stand, it's a dame that's drunk."

"We'll always have Paris."

"I stick my neck out for nobody."

"Round up the usual suspects."

2. Who among the following was **NOT** a member of
Hollywood's famous "Rat Pack"?

Frank Sinatra

Dean Martin

Jerry Lewis

Peter Lawford

Sammy Davis Jr.

3. What do the following actors have in common?

> Woody Allen
>
> Warren Beatty
>
> George Clooney
>
> Clint Eastwood
>
> Mel Gibson
>
> Gene Kelly

---

4. In Shakespeare's time, it was common for male actors to assume both male and female roles in the Bard's plays. Match up the following modern actors with movies in which they masqueraded as women:

1.	Ray Bolger	**A.**	*Tootsie*
2.	Tony Curtis	**B.**	*Some Like It Hot*
3.	Dustin Hoffman	**C.**	*Hairspray*
4.	Nathan Lane	**D.**	*Mrs. Doubtfire*
5.	John Travolta	**E.**	*Where's Charley?*
6.	Robin Williams	**F.**	*The Birdcage*

---

5. Name the famous film director whose signature
was making brief, nonspeaking cameo appearances
in each of his movies.

_____

6. Which of the following actors did **NOT** appear in any
film version of a Shakespearean play?
    Mel Gibson
    Kevin Kline
    Al Pacino
    Sean Penn
    Denzel Washington
    Orson Welles

_____

7. During the Johnny Carson years of *The Tonight Show*, several well-known personalities served as guest host. Which of the following filled in for Johnny the greatest number of times?

Jerry Lewis
Bob Newhart
Joey Bishop
Joan Rivers
David Brenner
David Letterman

Danzel?
orson?
mel?
Kevin?
AL?
Sean?

8. Match the following actors with the real people they portrayed on the silver screen:

1. Leonardo DiCaprio   **A.** Charlie Chaplin
2. Robert Downey Jr.   **B.** Charles Lindbergh
3. Charlton Heston   **C.** George M. Cohan
4. Jack Nicholson   **D.** Jimmy Hoffa
5. Brad Pitt   **E.** Howard Hughes
6. James Stewart   **F.** Michelangelo
7. James Cagney   **G.** Jesse James

_____

_____

_____

9. Two leading actors have played the life of composer Cole Porter in films named after two of his songs, *Night and Day* in 1946 and *De-Lovely* in 2004. Name the actors.

_____

_____

10. Actor Gary Burghoff was the only cast member of the 1970 film *M*A*S*H* to become a regular on the popular television series. Identify the role he played in both versions.

_____

11. Which of these women holds the record for most Academy Awards for best actress?

> Ingrid Bergman
> Bette Davis
> Jane Fonda
> Katharine Hepburn
> Meryl Streep
> Elizabeth Taylor

12. Which of these actors **NEVER** played British agent
James Bond on screen?

    Sean Connery
    Daniel Craig
    Timothy Dalton
    Hugh Grant
    George Lazenby
    Roger Moore
    David Niven

_____

13. A famous Oscar-winning film director holds the distinction of having directed Academy Award–winning performances by his father in *The Treasure of Sierra Madre* (1948) and his daughter in *Prizzi's Honor* (1985). Can you identify this talented theatrical trio?

    _____

    _____

    _____

14. Which of these films garnered the most Oscar nominations for a single picture?

    Gone with the Wind (1939)

    The Best Years of Our Lives (1946)

    Patton (1970)

    The Godfather: Part II (1974)

    Titanic (1997)

    Chicago (2002)

    _____

15. Name the actress who played the love interest of
the following leading men in different films:

    Nicolas Cage

    Russell Crowe

    Billy Crystal

    Tom Hanks

    Kevin Kline

    Hugh Jackman

_____

16. Aside from the fact that they were produced in the
same decade, what did these movie musicals have
in common?

    West Side Story (1961)

    My Fair Lady (1964)

    The Sound of Music (1965)

    Oliver! (1968)

_____

17. What successful Hollywood film director got his start in show business as an actor in two hugely popular TV comedy series, one as a child star and the other as a teen star?

_____

18. What do the following film stars have in common?

    Dan Aykroyd

    Joan Cusack

    Robert Downey Jr.

    Will Ferrell

    Eddie Murphy

    Ben Stiller

_____

19. Name the parent-offspring acting duos who appeared together in these films:

     Paper Moon (1973)
     On Golden Pond (1981)
     Wall Street (1987)
     It Runs in the Family (2003)
     The Pursuit of Happyness (2006)
     The Heartbreak Kid (2007)

_____

_____

_____

_____

_____

_____

20. What famous fictional character was played by each of these actors over the years?

     Alistair Sim (1951)
     Albert Finney (1970)
     George C. Scott (1984)
     Patrick Stewart (1999)
     Kelsey Grammer (2004)

_____

21. The Beatles made several rollicking full-length films together in the 1960s. What was the title of the very first one in 1964?

_____

22. What do these film actors have in common?
　　　Christian Bale
　　　George Clooney
　　　Michael Keaton
　　　Val Kilmer
　　　Adam West

_____

23. More than three dozen movies have been made from novels by this popular author, including _Carrie_ (1976), _Stand by Me_ (1986), _The Shawshank Redemption_ (1994); and _Secret Window_ (2004). Name the writer.

_____

24. Match the following actresses with characters they portrayed on screen:

1.	Vivien Leigh	**A.**	Norma Desmond
2.	Helen Mirren	**B.**	Erin Brockovich
3.	Julia Roberts	**C.**	Miss Daisy
4.	Gloria Swanson	**D.**	Queen Elizabeth II
5.	Jessica Tandy	**E.**	Maggie the Cat
6.	Elizabeth Taylor	**F.**	Scarlett O'Hara

_____

_____

_____

25. In eight decades of Academy Awards ceremonies, who hosted or cohosted the show more times than any other celebrity?

_____

Bookworm

Dust off your jacket and see if you can remember the ins and outs of these great books and their characters.

✳ **answers on pages 327–330**

I. Match the character with the novel:

1.	Holden Caulfield	**A.**	*The Grapes of Wrath* (John Steinbeck)
2.	Atticus Finch	**B.**	*The Catcher in the Rye* (J. D. Salinger)
3.	Lord Voldemort	**C.**	*To Kill a Mockingbird* (Harper Lee)
4.	Tom Joad	**D.**	*Great Expectations* (Charles Dickens)
5.	Pip	**E.**	*Harry Potter and the Sorcerer's Stone* (J. K. Rowling)

_____

_____

_____

2. Match the real names of these writers with
their pseudonyms:

1.	Eric Arthur Blair	**A.**	Mark Twain
2.	Samuel Clemens	**B.**	Richard Bachman
3.	Theodore Geisel	**C.**	George Orwell
4.	Stephen King	**D.**	O. Henry
5.	William Sydney Porter	**E.**	Dr. Seuss

_____

_____

_____

3. Name the only president of the United States to win a Pulitzer Prize for a book he wrote prior to his election.

_____

4. Which one of these authors has had the most novels turned into full-length feature films?

    Charles Dickens

    Nora Ephron

    John Grisham

    Stephen King

    John Steinbeck

_____

5. Which one of the following prolific authors **NEVER** wrote a detective or spy story?

    William F. Buckley

    Graham Greene

    Norman Mailer

    Dorothy Parker

    Edgar Allan Poe

_____

6. What do the following book titles have in common?

    Brave New World (Aldous Huxley)

    The Dogs of War (Frederick Forsyth)

    Perchance to Dream (Robert B. Parker)

    Pomp and Circumstance (Noël Coward)

    The Sound and the Fury (William Faulkner)

_____

_____

_____

7. Don't be fooled: Who wrote *The Autobiography of Alice B. Toklas?*

_____

8. By the numbers now, which writers wrote which books?

1. Ray Bradbury	**A.**	*Slaughterhouse-Five*
2. Joseph Heller	**B.**	*Fahrenheit 451*
3. George Orwell	**C.**	*The Hundred and*
4. Dodie Smith		*One Dalmatians*
5. Kurt Vonnegut	**D.**	*Catch-22*
	E.	*1984*

_____

_____

_____

9. Which of these African-American writers preceded all the others on this list?

Maya Angelou

Zora Neale Hurston

Toni Morrison

Alice Walker

Phyllis Wheatley

_____

10. Which one of the following writers on black themes is **NOT** himself African-American?

James Baldwin

Ralph Ellison

Alex Haley

William Styron

Richard Wright

_____

11. In May 2008, what phenomenally popular author did not have a book appearing in at least one category of the *New York Times* weekly best-seller lists for the first time in ten straight years?

_____

12. Fill in the missing initials:
1. __ __ Doctorow
2. __ Scott Fitzgerald
3. __ __ Mencken
4. __ __ __ Tolkien
5. __ __ White

13. Identify the all-time best-selling book still in print.

_____

14. On a list of "100 Best Novels" compiled by the Modern Library in 1998, books by James Joyce took two of the first three top spots. Name those books.

_____

_____

15. Here are five opening lines to famous novels. Identify the books and their authors:

1. "Call me Ishmael."

_____

_____

2. "It was a bright cold day in April, and the clocks were striking thirteen."

_____

_____

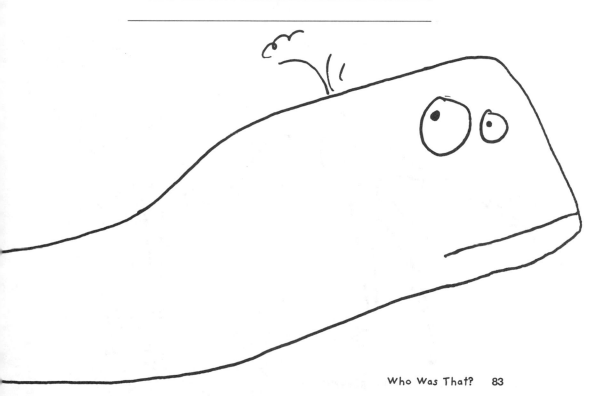

3. "Somewhere in La Mancha, in a place whose name I do not care to remember, a gentleman lived not long ago, one of those who has a lance and ancient shield on a shelf and keeps a skinny nag and a greyhound for racing."

_____

_____

4. "It was a pleasure to burn."

_____

_____

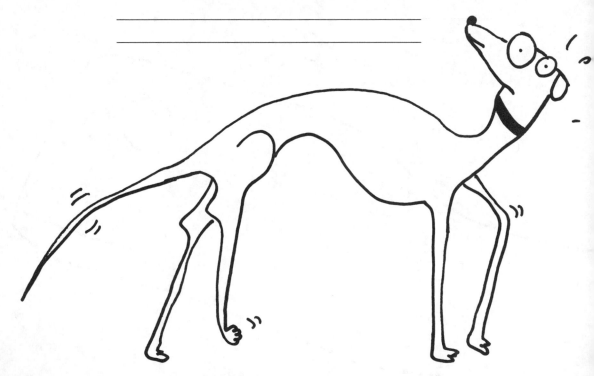

5. "If you really want to hear about it, the first thing you'll probably want to know is where I was born, and what my lousy childhood was like, and how my parents were occupied and all before they had me, and all that David Copperfield kind of crap, but I don't feel like going into it, if you want to know the truth."

_____

_____

16. From another novel by one of the authors listed in **Question 15,** what title character uttered these last words before being hanged? "God bless Captain Vere!"

_____

17. Link these Ernest Hemingway novels with the countries in which they were set:

1. *Across the River and into the Trees*
2. *A Farewell to Arms*
3. *For Whom the Bell Tolls*
4. *To Have and Have Not*
5. *The Old Man and the Sea*
6. *The Sun Also Rises*

A. Cuba
B. United States and Cuba
C. Spain
D. France and Spain
E. Italy
F. Italy and Switzerland

_____

_____

_____

18. Which one of the following superheroes did **NOT** originate as a comic-strip or comic-book character?

    Batman

    The Phantom

    Spider-man

    Superman

    Tarzan

19. Match the authors with their well-read "Red" books:

1.	Tom Clancy	**A.**	*The Red and the Black*
2.	Stephen Crane	**B.**	*The Red Pony*
3.	Wilson Rawls	**C.**	*The Little Red Book*
4.	John Steinbeck	**D.**	*The Hunt for Red October*
5.	Stendhal	**E.**	*Where the Red Fern Grows*
6.	Mao Tse-tung	**F.**	*The Red Badge of Courage*

20. On August 6, 1975, for the only time in its history, the *New York Times* published a front-page obituary of a popular fictional character to mark the release of *Curtain*, the last in a long series of books chronicling his adventures as a private detective. Can you name this singularly honored character?

_____

21. Name the hard-boiled Raymond Chandler detective portrayed variously in movies by Humphrey Bogart, Elliott Gould, Robert Mitchum, Robert Montgomery, and Dick Powell.

_____

22. Match the authors to the famous horror stories
they created:

1. *Dracula*
2. *Dr. Jekyll and Mr. Hyde*
3. *Frankenstein*
4. *The Hunchback of Notre Dame*
5. *The Invisible Man*
6. *Rosemary's Baby*

A. Mary Shelley
B. Victor Hugo
C. Bram Stoker
D. Ira Levin
E. Robert Louis Stevenson
F. H. G. Wells

_____

_____

_____

23. Most of the stories in the collected *Adventures of Sherlock Holmes* were told in the voice of his friend and assistant, Dr. John Watson. Two of the tales, however, were narrated by someone else. Which of the following characters was the other narrator?

1. Sherlock Holmes, himself

2. His older brother, Mycroft Holmes

3. His landlady, Mrs. Hudson

4. Another tenant at 221B Baker Street

5. Inspector Lestrade of Scotland Yard

---

24. What kind of animals mounted a Bolshevik-style revolution and took charge in George Orwell's allegorical novel, *Animal Farm*?

---

25. Link the following novels with the sports involved:

1. *For Love of the Game*   **A.** Tennis
2. *The Harder They Fall*   **B.** Golf
3. *The Hustler*   **C.** Baseball
4. *The Legend of*   **D.** Boxing
   Bagger Vance   **E.** Pool
5. *The Tournament*

_____

_____

_____

History Trivia

✳ answers on pages 331–333

I. When Abraham Lincoln opened his Gettysburg Address with the words "Fourscore and seven years ago . . . ," how many years was he referring to?

_____

2. What did these presidents have in common?

    Adams

    Johnson

    Harrison

    Roosevelt

    Bush

_____

3. Name the only man to serve as both U.S. vice president and president without having been elected to either office.

_____

4. In what Southern city was Martin Luther King Jr. assassinated on April 4, 1968?

_____

5. What are the first three words of the U.S. Constitution?

_____

6. In 1981, president Ronald Reagan appointed the Supreme Court's first female justice. She served for a quarter of a century until her retirement in 2006. Who is she?

_____

7. Which were the last two states to enter the Union? When were they admitted?

_____

_____

8. Identify the American general who was named supreme commander of allied forces in Europe during World War II?

_____

_____

9. Which of these astronauts was the first American in space?

    John Glenn

    Alan Shepard

    Neil Armstrong

_____

10. Who served as president of the Confederate States during the American Civil War?

_____

11. What three countries were characterized as an "axis of evil" by President George W. Bush in 2001?

_____

_____

_____

12. For which two European monarchs were the states of Louisiana and Virginia named?

_____

_____

13. Match the president with the appropriate slogan:

1.	Franklin D. Roosevelt	**A.**	New Frontier
2.	Harry Truman	**B.**	Morning in America
3.	John F. Kennedy	**C.**	New Deal
4.	Lyndon Johnson	**D.**	Fair Deal
5.	Ronald Reagan	**E.**	Compassionate Conservatism
6.	George W. Bush	**F.**	The Great Society

14. What name was given to the disastrous hurricane that flooded 80 percent of New Orleans in August 2005?

_____

15. Four presidents of the United States have had first and last names beginning with the same letter. How many can you name?

_____

_____

_____

_____

16. Charles Lindbergh made the first solo nonstop transatlantic flight in 1927. What was the name of his plane?

_____

17. In 1970, National Guards fired upon antiwar protesters at Kent State University, killing four students. In what state is Kent State?

_____

18. Who was the first and only president elected to three consecutive terms?

_____

19. What international organization, established in 1919 following World War I, served as an early version of the United Nations?

_____

20. The first ten amendments to the U.S. Constitution, proposed by the First Congress and ratified by the states in 1791, are collectively known by what title?

_____

21. Match these presidents with their middle names:

1. Franklin Roosevelt
2. Dwight Eisenhower
3. John Kennedy
4. Lyndon Johnson
5. Richard Nixon
6. Gerald Ford
7. James Carter
8. Ronald Reagan
9. William Clinton
10. George Bush

A. Milhous
B. Earl
C. Rudolph
D. Walker
E. Fitzgerald
F. Delano
G. Jefferson
H. Baines
I. Wilson
J. David

_____

_____

_____

_____

22. In 1903, the Wright Brothers went airborne with the first controlled, powered flight in a heavier-than-air craft, ushering in the Age of Flight. Where did they conduct their "flying machine" experiments?

_____

23. The U.S. House of Representatives has voted to impeach a president only twice in the nation's history. Both were brought to trial and both acquitted by the U.S. Senate. Name the two presidents.

_____

_____

24. What two prominent American sites were struck by terrorist-hijacked commercial jetliners on September 11, 2001?

_____

_____

25. How many of the thirteen original states can you name?

_____

_____

_____

_____

_____

_____

_____

_____

_____

_____

_____

_____

Memory Box #2

Feeling adrift or lost at sea when someone asks you what you did last night? Dive on in to this visual puzzle and revive that memory!

Take a close look at the images on this page. Give yourself a minute. Then, turn the page and see how many questions you can answer.

* answers on page 333

1. Were most fish facing left or right?

   _____

2. How many fish did **NOT** have stripes?

   _____

3. How many scuba divers were there?

   _____

4. What animal was squirting the walrus?

   _____

5. How many clams were there?

   _____

6. Was it noon or afternoon?

   _____

7. Was the wind blowing East or West?

_____

8. How many anchors were there?

_____

9. Did the sea anemones have dark or light "faces"?

_____

10. What kind of shark was in the picture?

_____

Chapter Three:

WHAT WAS THAT, AGAIN?

These puzzlers take the familiar and mix it up so your brain will have to work a little harder to get the right answer. Novel approaches will push your brain to move beyond how it's been working over time, and will spark your cognitive reserve. Arm yourself against the inevitable slowing that faces us all.

Dust off your cerebral spell-check and take a crack at finding misspelled wurds. Rearrange words to make a familiar phrase and unscramble some famous and funny quotes.

In Other Words

Idioms are commonly known phrases that make their way into our day-to-day speech and thinking. Here are some common sayings that have been rewritten. Can you translate them?

✳ answers on pages 334–335

I. Can you identify the following common offer?

This nominal American fiscal unit is offered in exchange for personal cerebral activity.

_____

_____

2. What is this descriptive phrase that might be used to describe Benji?

The vociferous nature of his being is far more intense than the physical act of mastication.

_____

_____

3. This is something Billie Jean King must have said.

The sphere has arrived and is contained within your enclosed official recreational area.

_____

_____

4. What are these two idioms based on a Simon and Garfunkel structure staple?

You and I might span the overpass upon reaching that destination.

_____

_____

Do not ignite the viaducts.

_____

_____

5. Or so Charles thinks . . .

The dwelling of a hominid is a secular
architectural stronghold.

_____

_____

6. Colonel Sanders never does this . . .

Poultry calculation prior to emergence
from the calcareous covering.

_____

7. John James Audubon probably agrees with these:

A single bipedal, warm-blooded, egg-laying vertebrate in a prehensile grasp has a double value than when in shrubbery.

_____

_____

_____

_____

Aves with similar plumage gather in groups.

_____

_____

8. Can you translate this beastly saying?

No glancing into the oral orifice of the donated equine.

_____

_____

9. What are these corporal proverbs?

Maintain intersected manual digits.

_____

_____

Self-snout slicing? Not so much.

_____

_____

10. Proverb Dear Abby might have said:

Failed amorous activity is preferred to none at all.

_____

_____

11. From *Dancing with the Stars* . . .

For a sassy Argentine dance, it is required to have a pair of dancers.

_____

_____

12. True for Ray Charles . . .

Passionate adoration is ocular-deficient.

_____

_____

13. Willard Scott motto:

Drizzly precipitation evaporate! Resume activity on an alternative period of sunlight.

_____

_____

14. Shhhhhh!

Gilded is the lack of din.

_____

_____

15. We're not talking corn, here:

That which holds up the ceiling also possesses
aural organs.

_____

_____

16. Probably not a practical idea:

Attack infernos with a combustible
heat-producing reaction.

_____

_____

17. A spelunker's creed:

    Illumination appears in faraway channel entries.

    _____

    _____

    And a spelunker's nightmare:

    Glowing emanates from within though
    the habitude seems deserted.

    _____

    _____

18. Two for the Gipper:

    Activity that produces no aches is
    not productive.

    _____

    _____

    After a failed primary attempt, endeavor
    multiple times.

    _____

    _____

19. It's about time:

Primarily on the occasion when the lunar
satellite has an azure appearance.

_____

_____

For the duration of the event upon
which the bovine ungulates return to their
dwelling place.

_____

_____

20. Julia Child's standby:

Soaring temperatures drive the intolerant
from food-preparation areas.

_____

_____

21. Father knows best:

      The measure of passing moments is fleeting.

_____

_____

22. Trump this!

      Legal tender performs discourse.

_____

_____

23. Realtor's fear:

Calcium-based bony frame within a small enclosed storage space with a door.

_____

_____

24. Just ask a mosquito:

The body's circulation fluid has more viscosity than that which flows from the tap.

_____

_____

25. Johnny Depp would know:

What's the policy of dealing with an inebriated man of the sea?

_____

_____

The deceased impart no fiction.

_____

_____

Scramblers—Famous Quotes, Titles, Etc.

Can you unscramble the order of these words to come up with a well-known quote?

✳ answers on pages 336–338

1. "The soul brevity is of lingerie." DOROTHY PARKER

_____

2. "Good father surgeon looks. From her he's she got her a plastic." GROUCHO MARX

_____

3. "As money as respectable has never been virtue."
MARK TWAIN

_____

4. "She a someone on who developed a troubled
persistent expression with repair is trying to watch his
which gave her the frown of gloves." JAMES THURBER

_____

_____

What Was That, Again?   123

5. "I'm afraid it's just I don't die when it happens there. To want to be not that." WOODY ALLEN

_____

_____

6. "And for a man hanging good puns should be quoted. He who is too makes drawn." FRED ALLEN

_____

7. "About talked only about worse thing the talked being than is not being." OSCAR WILDE

_____

8. "Up to have my father's father's father's contempt for my father's walk looks, speech patterns, my posture, father's opinions and I grew my my my, my mother's father." JULES FEIFFER

_____

_____

_____

_____

_____

9. "Experience men never learn anything that we learn from from experience." GEORGE BERNARD SHAW

_____

_____

10. "Cooked like properly children. I they're if."
W. C. FIELDS

_____

_____

11. "For today yesterday tomorrow I was a dog dog.
Dog I'm a little advancement. I'll probably still be a.
Sigh! so there's hope." SNOOPY (CHARLES SCHULZ)

_____

_____

_____

_____

12. "Easy distance brave it safe is to be from a." AESOP

_____

_____

13. "Early man makes a bed to rise early and to wise healthy, wealthy, and." Benjamin Franklin

_____

_____

14. "Past I think over, the we agree is." George W. Bush

_____

_____

What Was That, Again?   127

15. "Regulated accidents occur will in families the best."
CHARLES DICKENS

_____

_____

16. "Apart by men are wide nearly alike; by nature,
practice, they get to be." CONFUCIUS

_____

_____

17. "Be about reading books careful misprint.
You may die of a health." MARK TWAIN

_____

_____

18. "If have you, it virtue assume not a."
WILLIAM SHAKESPEARE

_____

_____

19. "A lifetime of bear hell happiness! No earth alive on man could be it; it would." GEORGE BERNARD SHAW

_____

_____

20. "Right if you're on the you'll get over even run if you just track, sit there." WILL ROGERS

_____

_____

21. "Go, again and darken my never towels."
GROUCHO MARX

_____

_____

22. "A strong woman is a hot bag—you water she never tea like know how is until she gets in."
ELEANOR ROOSEVELT

_____

_____

23. "Books without I cannot live." THOMAS JEFFERSON

_____

_____

24. "In the preservation is the world of wildness."
HENRY DAVID THOREAU

_____

_____

25. "Me hate what you know. I tell quotations."
RALPH WALDO EMERSON

_____

_____

1. Although Bill's accordion playing was strictly amatuer, Sheila, the champion professional polka dancer, still found him generally irresistible.

_____

2. Colonel Hardy vigorously defended the judgment of his battalion commander as a matter of principal.

_____

3. Janet commandeered the vaccuum cleaner and began desperately extracting dirt particles from the rug.

_____

4. Upon returning home from the cemetary, family members raised a glass of Grandma's favorite drink, a daiquiri, to her memory.

_____

5. The boy tried to cover his embarrassment by explaining that his spontaneous outburst was inadvertant and without forethought.

_____

6. Craving his first decent meal since completing a jail term for drunkenness, Ronald demanded to be driven to the best resturant in town.

_____

7. When the office secretaries took a break, their favorite passtime was to concoct a phony questionnaire incorporating racy remarks about the company's products.

_____

8. Dear Miss Bliss: Please disregard my most recent missive, which was full of mistakes. I even mispelled your name, based on misinformation and a missing address book. Sincerely, Mister Mossbrain.

_____

9. My dear Mossbrain: Don't worry, any offense taken by me would be minuscule and even irrelevant since I never recieved the letter in question. Best, Chris Bliss.

_____

10. The police allowed witnesses to leave the crime scene, but only after gathering indispensable data about them, such as heighth, width, shoe size, and blood protein type.

_____

11. Throughout his long life, Angelo tried many varied careers, from plumber to playwrite, from ornithologist to jewelry designer.

_____

12. Sarah's favorite aunt gave her this advice for getting the most out of life: "Follow your instincts, persue your dreams, and always seize the moment!"

_____

13. In his speech, the nation's drug czar said use of an enhanced version of the illegal hallucinogen ecstacy might lead to toxic effects on the brain and hyperthermia.

_____

14. By the time people reach fourty, their eyes begin to weaken; by sixty they have achiness in their bones; and at eighty they may snooze a lot.

_____

15. Jason's parents foresaw a scientific future for him because of his passion in school for physics, mathmatics, and chemistry.

_____

16. While at the market, Mother noticed that while her shopping list included broccoli, cantaloupe, razberries, and pistachios, she had forgotten to include cauliflower, my favorite veggie.

_____

17. In medieval times, sorcerors were sometimes considered to be instruments of sacrilege and heretical agents of the devil.

_____

18. Wanting a memento of their trip to the Italian peninsula, the Baileys brought back a bottle of local wine as a souvernir.

_____

19. When the septuagenarian and the octogenarian stood paralell to each other, they both gave the appearance of being the same or similar age.

_____

20. Jessica was well known for her firey personality and ability to intimidate anyone who impetuously challenged her veracity.

_____

21. When the stranger attempted to sieze Amy in his arms, she nimbly ducked and eluded his fumbling grasp.

_____

22. To say that the existence of a short story with similar characters constituted plagerism by Adam was more than the judge would accept.

_____

23. First, the mayor appointed an inept nephew as his principal assistant; then he annointed his own privileged son as his successor.

_____

24. The unyielding leader of the western expedition was determined that the emigrants procede on schedule, even when the supply wagon's axle showed dangerous signs of wear.

_____

25. The likelihood of Lincoln leading a liesurely life was not deemed legitimate by his fellow legislators.

_____

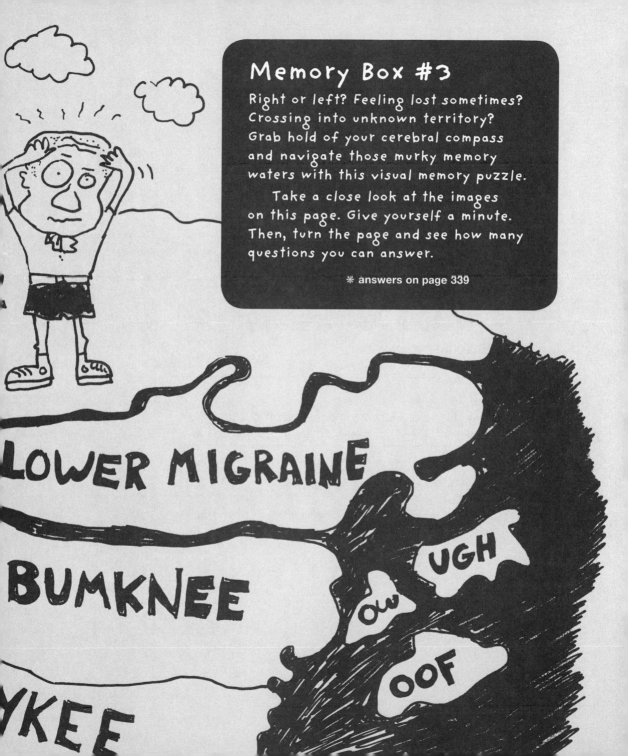

1. Name the three islands.

   _____

2. Which country had mountains?

   _____

3. Can you name the four coastal countries?

   _____

4. Which country has rivers as north and
   south boders?

   _____

5. Is Napz or Flakovia the westernmost country?

   _____

6. Which two countries had trees?

   _____

7. If you started in Upper Migraine and went west, which country would you come to first?

    _____

8. Which island is off the coast of Bumknee?

    _____

9. If you were in southern Napz and took a road trip south, where would you end up?

    _____

10. The clouds are over which country?

    _____

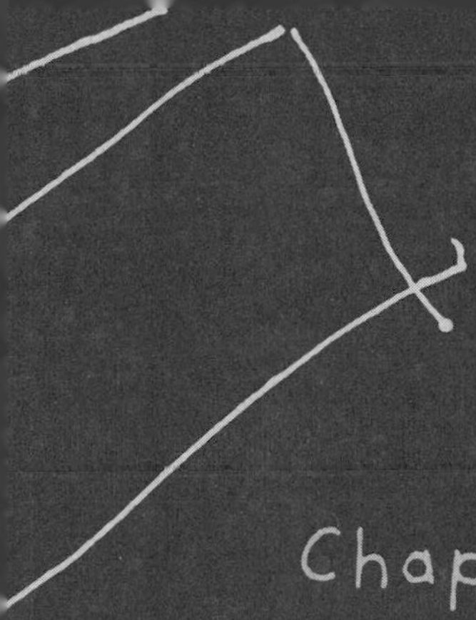

Chapter Four:

WORD SURGERY

When you get to be a certain age, words go flying out of your brain faster than a chicken from a coop. Here's some help.

Nip a letter here, tuck one in there. Give your vocabulary and word recognition a little lift! You'll think ten years younger!

Word Transformers

With each step, change only one letter to transform one word into another. The first one is done for you. (The number of lines matches the number of steps.)

✻ answers on pages 340–342

1. **TIE to LEG**

   TIE
   PIE
   PIG
   PEG
   LEG

2. **HEAD to FOOT**

   HEAD

   _____

   _____

   _____

   FOOT

3. GIFT to LOVE

GIFT

_____

_____

_____

LOVE

4. WET to DRY

WET

_____

_____

_____

_____

DRY

5. OLD to NEW

OLD

_____

_____

_____

_____

_____

_____

NEW

6. BOOM to HEAR

BOOM

_____

_____

_____

HEAR

7. HARD to EASY

HARD

_____

_____

_____

_____

EASY

8. NORTH to SOUTH

NORTH

_____

_____

_____

_____

_____

SOUTH

9. **ARM to LEG**

ARM

_____

_____

_____

_____

LEG

10. **SLEEP to DREAM**

SLEEP

_____

_____

_____

_____

_____

DREAM

11. **TOP to GUN**

TOP

_____

_____

_____

GUN

12. **HOT to LIP**

HOT

_____

_____

LIP

13. **HIP to JOG**

HIP

_____

_____

JOG

14. ARE to OUT

ARE

_____

_____

_____

OUT

15. CAT to DOG

CAT

_____

_____

DOG

16. HOT to NUN

HOT

_____
_____
_____
_____
_____

NUN

17. STARE to TEARS

STARE

_____

_____

TEARS

18. FIRE to FOUL

FIRE

_____

_____

_____

_____

FOUL

19. PAWN to KING

PAWN

_____

_____

_____

_____

_____

KING

20. BLURT to SHARE

BLURT

_____

_____

_____

_____

_____

SHARE

21. SEED to GROW

SEED

_____

_____

_____

_____

GROW

22. GREEN to GRASS

GREEN

_____

_____

_____

_____

_____

_____

GRASS

23. TREE to FALL

TREE

_____

_____

_____

_____

_____

FALL

24. COOK to FOOD

COOK

_____

_____

FOOD

25. WARM to COLD

WARM

_____

_____

_____

_____

COLD

Shrinky-Thinks

In each of the following sentences, there are two clues. Find the word represented by the first clue and then subtract one letter to get the word corresponding to the second clue.

✳ answers on page 343

Example:

Take the espresso drink Bob lingered over and get his failure to arrive to work on time.

(**ANSWER:** *LATTE/LATE*)

I. Take the forty-third President and give him one way to get out of town.

    _____/_____

2. Take this golfer and get a higher level.

    _____/_____

3. Ken pronounced this evening meal first-rate.

_____/_____

4. You could have knocked Alice over with one of these when this relative arrived unannounced.

_____/_____

5. Take what firmly tied the astronaut to the capsule and get what he ventured into in space.

_____/_____

6. Take what happened to Judy when she accidentally stepped on a bee and get how she hit her high C.

   _____/_____

7. Take this monarch and make him a part of your family tree.

   _____/_____

8. Take Sondra's physical attractiveness and get how she alienated friends by gossiping about their minor shortcomings.

   _____/_____

9. Take this European capital city and get a pile of regulation golf scores on several holes.

   _____/_____

10. Take what the country priest did on his bike and get how the church bell prompted him to do so.

   _____/_____

11. Take your muscular tasting organ and get a fresh-water fish that may or may not appeal to it.

_____/_____

12. Take the source of intellectual power and get this dietary fiber that keeps your body healthy.

_____/_____

13. Take the audience's quivering delight and get the purity of the soprano's vibrato that brought them to a standing ovation.

_____/_____

14. A cheese dealer's credo: Take this strong odor and get the secret of market success.

_____/_____

15. Take this common bakery product and get a welcome intellect-stimulating pastime.

_____/_____

16. Take this American holiday and get how it signifies the nation's advance.

_____/_____

17. Take the gift Ed gave to the lady next door and get her husband's negative reaction.

_____/_____

18. Take this jet operator and get how the terrorist used him as part of this scheme.

_____/_____

19. Take Jason's involvement in a highway accident and see what it cost his insurance company.

_____/_____

20. Take the charm Sarah wore suspended from a chain around her neck and get what she became while teaching a course in Native American culture.

_____/_____

21. Take this popular dried fruit and get a character of an ancient alphabet.

_____/_____

22. Take this figure of speech in which two unlike things are explicitly compared and get this facial sign of appreciative pleasure.

_____/_____

23. Take this small tree branch and get this fine head of hair.

_____/_____

24. Take an old heroic tale and get what can happen to a listener if it goes on for too long.

_____/_____

25. Take this small rodent and get a Disney inspiration.

_____/_____

Lop the Top

Drop the first letter off to make a new word. Here's an example to get you started.

❋ answers on page 344

Take the first letter off this part of a car and get the bottom of your shoe.
(wheel/heel)

1. Take the first letter off this illegal action and get a bridesmaid's gown color.

    _____/_____

2. Take the first letter off this thing people do to sheep and listen up.

    _____/_____

3. Take the first letter off this trumpet action and get a bass sound.

_____/_____

4. Take the first letter off this sound a gown makes and get something folks do when they see shooting stars.

_____/_____

5. Take the first letter off the fairer sex and get a warning sign.

_____/_____

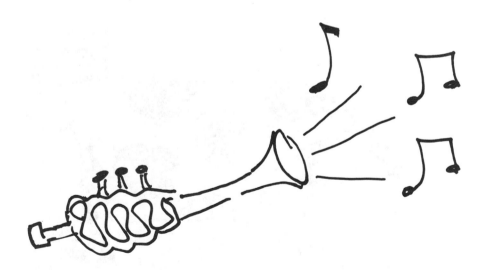

6. Take the first letter off this winter essential and get what we're all looking for.

_____/_____

7. Take the first letter off this reproductive part of an angiosperm and don't get higher.

_____/_____

8. Take the first letter off this sandwich staple and do this to a book.

_____/_____

9. Take the first letter off this protein food and tuck right in.

   _____/_____

10. Take the first letter off this metric mass unit and get the symbol of Aries.

    _____/_____

11. Take the first letter off this fatty dairy product and hollow something out.

    _____/_____

12. Take the first letter off this impulse and get "that guy."

    _____/_____

13. Take the first letter off this smudge and get Noah's big project.

    _____/_____

14. Take the first letter off this home to horses and get some real height.

_____/_____

15. Take the first letter off this yard tool and get a ramshackle abode.

_____/_____

16. Take the first letter off this means of astonishment and get a labyrinth.

_____/_____

17. Take the first letter off your footwear and get digging in the garden.

_____ / _____

18. Take the first letter off this grain and get a high temperature.

_____ / _____

19. Take the first letter off this place to run in circles and get a place to hang your hat.

_____ / _____

20. Take the first letter off this final resting place and get a wild dance party.

_____/_____

21. Take the first letter off this flower and start weaving on this.

_____/_____

22. Take the first letter off slow-witted and get a country bumpkin.

_____/_____

23. Take the first letter off this long bath and get the mighty acorn's dream.

_____/_____

24. Take the first letter off this ceiling holder and get everything.

_____/_____

25. Take the first letter off this thing to rise above and get a drop of golden sun.

_____/_____

INFLAMMATION   Arthur Itis

Container Gardens   by Clay Potz

Fake It   by Artie Fishel

LET IT POUR   by Wayne Dwops

SICK!   by Ann Thrax

CROCK   by Ali Gator

Job Search   by Anita Job

I was FLOORED   by Lynn O'Liam

SHOCKER!   by Alec Tricity

...   by Tim Burr

Memory Box #4

Quick! What's your favorite book? And who were the main characters in *Wuthering Heights*? Why did I buy this book? Missing some memory pages? Who isn't? Brush up your book-smarts with this visual memory puzzle.

Take a close look at the images on this page. Give yourself a minute. Then, turn the page and see how many questions you can answer.

✳ answers on page 345

LOOK Younger! by Fay Sifft

Neither a Borrower by Nora Lenbobee

I Love fish! by Ann Chovey

Dull Pain
A. King

You Can Help!
by
Abel N. Willing

Tight Squeeze by Leah Tard

Full Moon by Seymour Bunnz

1. How many books are there?

   _____

2. What's the title of the thickest book?

   _____

3. Who wrote *Let It Pour*?

   _____

4. What did Leah Tard write?

   _____

5. Who wrote *I Was Floored!*?

   _____

6. What did Artie Fishal write?

   _____

7. Who wrote *Inflammation*?

_____

8. Name the author of *Dull Pain*.

_____

9. Who penned *Sick!*?

_____

10. What did Nora Lenderbee write?

_____

Chapter Five

THAT'S A DIFFERENT WAY TO LOOK AT IT

Puns can make you groan. They can also spark the old noodle. This section is crammed with them—both visual and verbal. Scrambled anagrams and literal images make for some fun cortex carousing as they force you to think out of the box to solve the puzzles.

Anagrams

An anagram is a word or phrase that can be rearranged to make another word or phrase. In each of the following exercises, use all the letters to figure out the famous person each phrase is hiding. See the example below.

✳ answers on pages 345–347

RAW ROPE BIN
(BRAINPOWER)

ATHLETES

1. IM MADAM HULA

_____

2. REHAB TUB

_____

3. GOT SO WIRED

_____

4. MAJOR NICHE LAD

_____

5. JOINS MOPS

_____

POLITICAL FIGURES

1. CHILLY LOIN RANT

   _____

2. HE BUGS GORE

   _____

3. CHECKED YIN

   _____

4. MY METRIC JAR

   _____

5. CAPE IS NYLON

   _____

ACTORS

1. COOL EGO ENERGY

   _____

2. ME GIN SLOB

   _____

3. OLD WEST ACTION

   _____

4. MY HUED PRIDE

   _____

5. ANGRY ME

   _____

SINGERS

1. I BAWD VIDEO

   _____

2. PELVISES RELY

   _____

3. AND MOAN

   _____

4. CALM NOSE HIJACK

   _____

5. CRAM KEG JIG

   _____

AUTHORS

1. WINE ENRAGES MYTH

   _____

2. WARM AT INK

   _____

3. SHH MINOR JAG

   _____

4. OR MANLIER MAN

   _____

5. FLOW TOME

   _____

COMEDIANS

1. MADDER NAVEL TIT

    _____

2. MAIN BOIL SWIRL

    _____

3. HEP BOOB

    _____

4. NAIVEST TERM

    _____

5. BLURRY MAIL

    _____

HISTORICAL FIGURES

1. O REBEL TREE

   _____

2. RANCOR HID NIX

   _____

3. LA NEON OP

   _____

4. OH CHERUBIC SLUM PORTS

   _____

5. LOOSE VOTE LEARNER

   _____

COMPOSER-SONGWRITERS

1. A RUMPLY ACCENT

    _____

2. ACORN AND OPAL

    _____

3. HER SWING *

    _____

4. BLAND BOY

    _____

5. PERT COOLER

    _____

*Last name only

ARTISTS

1. BASIC ALSO POP

   _____

2. KNOWN CREAM ROLL

   _____

3. OLD VINO RADIANCE

   _____

4. THY DREW ANEW

   _____

5. EASEL COLOUR TUTU *

   _____

*Last name only

FOREIGN LEADERS

1. A COLD STRIFE

   _____

2. THE EQUINE BLAZE

   _____

3. HANDED US AMISS

   _____

4. ILL OF HATRED

   _____

5. SOBERLY I SNIT

   _____

Rebuses

Many 18th-century Americans amused themselves by writing rebus letters—where pictures represented words. Decode these modern-day rebus puzzlers and feel the clever spirit of colonies crackling in your contemporary cranium.

✳ answers on page 347

1. REBUS #1

2. REBUS #2

3. REBUS #3

H + O + 8   ♪ — EIGH

— LTE + DGE

— IL + AE

4. REBUS #4

5. REBUS #5

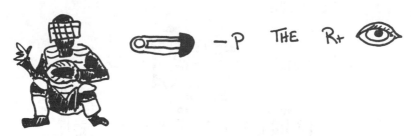

— P   THE   R+ 👁

6. REBUS #6

7. REBUS #7

8. REBUS #8

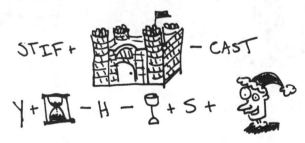

9. **REBUS #9**

Y + 🐰 — rit + a

D + 🐰 — rit + a 🐕 " + O − G

10. **REBUS #10**

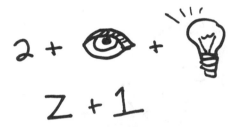

2 + 👁 + 💡

Z + 1

11. **REBUS #11**

👁 + M   🚫 C + 🪣

12. REBUS #12

13. REBUS #13

14. REBUS #14

15. REBUS #15

 + MER

16. REBUS #16

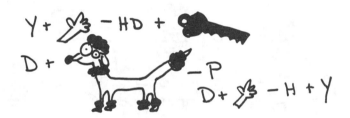

17. REBUS #17

T +

18. REBUS #18

 H + 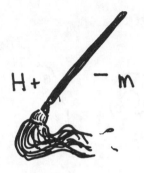 − m

19. REBUS #19

20. REBUS #20

N +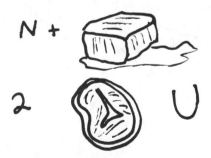

2 U

Word Pictures

If a picture is worth a thousand words, how about a few words that do double duty as visual puzzles? The first one is done for you.

✳ answers on page 348

I. STAND

  I

  I understand

2. VA DERS

  _____

3. GIVE, GIVE, GIVE, GIVE
  GET, GET, GET, GET

  _____

4. FAREDCE

  _____

5. TRAIL
RAILT
IALTR
AILRT

_____

6. 2. BLAME
3. BLAME

_____

7. LLA

_____

8. DOCTOR DOCTOR

_____

9. NAFISH
NAFISH

_____

10. ANOTHER ONE THING

_____

11. HISTORY HISTORY HISTORY

_____

12. MILL1ON

_____

13.   BUT
      THOUGHT   THOUGHT

_____

14. D
R
A
H

_____

15. HEAD
HEELS

_____

16. JOBINJOB

_____

17. E C O N O M Y

_____

18. TRY   STAND
             2

_____

19. THE PAAWALKRK

_____

20. . _____

_____

21. ARREST
    YOU'RE

_____

22. RIGHT ME

_____

23. TAKE TAKE

_____

24. TIME TIME

_____

25. BIRD

_____

Picture This

These drawings are whimsical illustrations of literal things. It's a real right-brain/left-brain exercise. Can you figure out what words or phrases they represent?

✴ answers on page 349

1.

2.

3.

4.

5.

6.

7.

8.

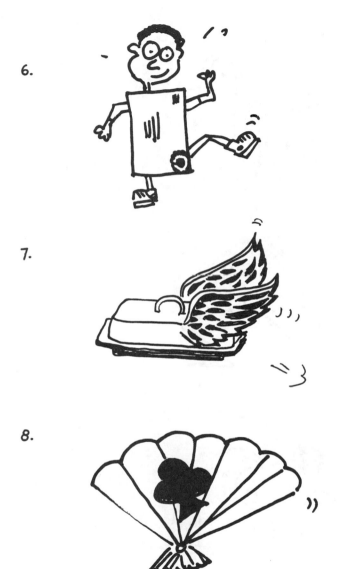

9.

10.

11.

12.

13.

14.

15.

16.

17.

18.

19.

20.

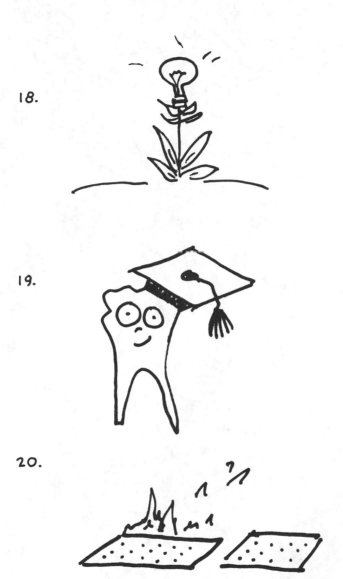

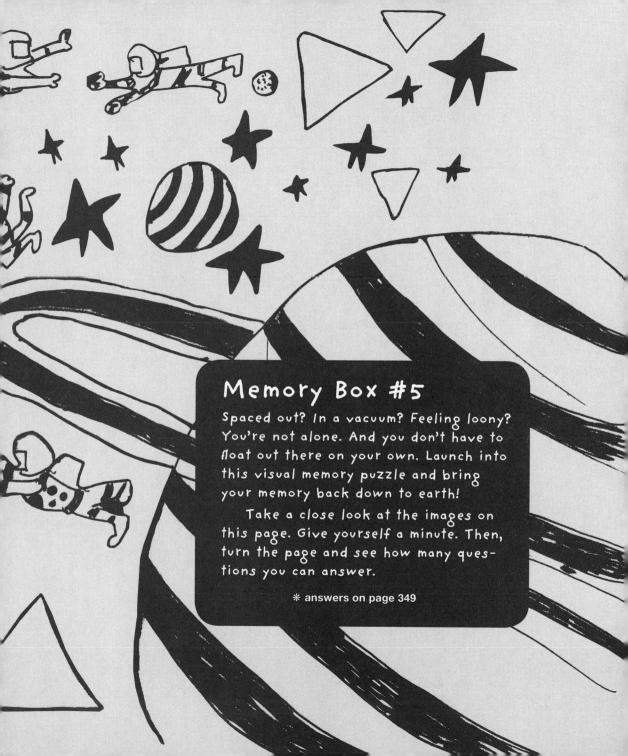

Memory Box #5

Spaced out? In a vacuum? Feeling loony? You're not alone. And you don't have to float out there on your own. Launch into this visual memory puzzle and bring your memory back down to earth!

Take a close look at the images on this page. Give yourself a minute. Then, turn the page and see how many questions you can answer.

※ answers on page 349

1. How many stars were there?

    _____

2. Were there more striped planets or spotted planets?

    _____

3. How many planets had rings?

    _____

4. Was the rocket headed for a striped planet?

    _____

5. How many astronauts were there?

    _____

6. Were there more astronauts facing left or right?

    _____

7. How many jets did the rocket have?

_____

8. Was the biggest planet striped or spotted?

_____

9. Was the smallest planet striped?

_____

10. How many spots did the lower left planet have?

_____

Chapter Six:

WHAT
DO YOU
KNOW?

It's not just what you know but how you make connections among the things you know. In this section the challenge is to discover the connections first and then either match them up, as in Mix Up Match, or find out what doesn't belong, as in Find the Misfit.

MIX UP MATCH

Can you figure out why these two columns are connected and how they match up?

* answers on pages 350–363

I.
Grey's Anatomy	Queens
WKRP	Cincinnati
Cheers	Milwaukee
Friends	New York
All in the Family	Boston
Laverne & Shirley	Seattle

_____

_____

_____

_____

_____

_____

2.

porcine	Felix
equine	Mr. Ed
canine	Pluto
feline	Porky

_____

_____

_____

_____

3.

King	Bigalow
Queen	London
Jack	Tut
Ace	Latifah
Deuce	Ventura

_____

_____

_____

_____

4. "Can you hear me now?"   McDonalds

"I'm lovin' it!"   Coca-Cola

"Love the skin you're in."   Dove

"My life. My card."   Verizon

"It's the real thing."   American Express

_____

_____

_____

_____

_____

5. porifera   The Simpsons
hominid   Charlotte
ungulate   Mickey Mouse
arachnid   Rudolph the Red-Nosed
rodent   Reindeer
SpongeBob SquarePants

_____

_____

_____

_____

_____

6. Catherine   *Love in the Time of Cholera*

Isabel   *The Old Man and the Sea*

Nick   *Portrait of a Lady*

Tom   *The Great Gatsby*

Santiago   *Wuthering Heights*

Florentino   *The Grapes of Wrath*

_____

_____

_____

_____

_____

7. Grandpa   Blonde

Herman   Frankenstein's monster

Eddie   Vampire

Spot   Fire-breathing dragon

Marilyn   Werewolf

_____

_____

_____

_____

_____

8. Wilbur   mouse

Buck   dog

Mickey   pig

Kermit   rabbit

George   frog

Misty   pony

Peter   monkey

_____

_____

_____

_____

_____

_____

_____

9. Holden   *To Kill a Mockingbird*

    Pip   *Gone with the Wind*

    Scarlett   *Great Expectations*

    Scout   *The House of Mirth*

    Selden   *Catcher in the Rye*

_____

_____

_____

_____

_____

10. Jo   *Little House on the Prairie*

    Hester   *Treasure Island*

    Jim   *The Scarlet Letter*

    Laura   *A Christmas Carol*

    Ebenezer   *Little Women*

_____

_____

_____

_____

_____

11. Jerry   Hot Lips
      Hawkeye   Darrin
      Chandler   Elaine
      Niles   Maris
      Tabitha   Monica

_____

_____

_____

_____

_____

12. Democratic Republic
of Congo

Benin

Burkina Faso

Lesotho

Botswana

Zimbabwe

Rhodesia

Dahomey

Bechuanaland

Upper Volta

Zaire

Basutoland

_____

_____

_____

_____

_____

_____

13. *Fred Basset*   Chic and Dean Young

     Garfield   Bill Watterson

     Dilbert   Scott Adams

     Blondie   Jim Davis

     Calvin and Hobbes   Alex Graham

_____

_____

_____

_____

_____

14. Brad   Katie

     Tom   Spencer

     Humphrey   Lucy

     Desi   Lauren

     Katharine   Angelina

_____

_____

_____

_____

_____

15. Johnny Hart   *Andy Capp*

Chester Gould   *Archie*

Reg Smythe   *B.C.*

Charles Schulz   *Dick Tracy*

Bob Montana   *Peanuts*

_____

_____

_____

_____

_____

16. "Never mind."

"I'm Gumby dammit!"

"It's better to look

    fabulous than

    to feel fabulous."

"Isn't that special?"

"Now is the time

    on Sprockets

    vhen ve dance!"

"Jane, you ignorant slut."

Mike Myers

Dana Carvey

Gilda Radner

Dan Akroyd

Eddie Murphy

Billy Crystal

_____

_____

_____

_____

_____

17. "I'm a little *verklempt*."

"You could be living in
a van, down by
the river."

"Buh BYE!"

"Acting!"

"Cheeburger, cheeburger,
cheeburger . . .
Pepsipepsipepsi!"

"Base-a-ball been a berra
berra good to me."

Garrett Morris

John Belushi

David Spade

Mike Myers

Jon Lovitz

Chris Farley

_____

_____

_____

_____

_____

_____

18. Orson Bean   Archibald Alexander Leach
     Jack Benny   Leslie Hornby
     Whoopi Goldberg   Caryn Elaine Johnson
     Cary Grant   Benjamin Kubelsky
     Twiggy   Dallas Frederick Burrows

_____

_____

_____

_____

_____

19. Col.   Plum

Miss   Peacock

Mr.   Green

Professor   Mustard

Mrs.   Scarlet

_____

_____

_____

_____

_____

20. Herman   Louise

Mike   Edith

Archie   Debra

Ray   Carol

Paul   Jamie

George   Lily

_____

_____

_____

_____

_____

21. Mick   Aerosmith

       Gordon   Police

       Paul   Van Halen

       David   U2

       Steven   Rolling Stones

_____

_____

_____

_____

_____

22. Gladys   Teenagers
Smokey   Supremes
Diana   Romans
Franky   Miracles
Little Caesar   Pips

_____

_____

_____

_____

_____

23. KC   E Street Band
Bob   Wailers
Bruce   Raiders
Bruce   Sunshine Band
Paul   Range

_____

_____

_____

_____

_____

24. Roger   Grateful Dead

Paul   The Who

Freddie   KISS

Jerry   Queen

_____

_____

_____

_____

25. Bono   Reginald

Sting   Marvin

Elton   Richard

Ringo   Gordon

Sonny   Paul

Meat Loaf   Salvatore

_____

_____

_____

_____

_____

_____

26. Woody Allen   Betty Joan Perske

Alan Alda   Alphonso Joseph D'Abruzzo

Bea Arthur   Frederick Austerlitz

Fred Astaire   Allen Stewart Konigsberg

Lauren Bacall   Bernice Frankel

_____

_____

_____

_____

_____

27. Siam   Sri Lanka

Formosa   Taiwan

Ceylon   Iraq

Hellas   Iran

Persia   Thailand

Mesopotamia Greece

_____

_____

_____

_____

_____

_____

28.

Julius	Rockets
Kareem	Lakers
Larry	Celtics
Michael	Knicks
Patrick	76ers
Hakeem	Jazz
John	Bulls

_____

_____

_____

_____

_____

_____

_____

29. Valencia   cherry

     Rainier   apple

     Fuji   orange

     Bosc   grape

     Concord   pear

_____

_____

_____

_____

_____

30. Georgia   pineapple

     Maine   orange

     Florida   blueberry

     California   apple

     Washington   peach

     Massachusetts   cranberry

     Hawaii   raisin

_____

_____

_____

_____

_____

_____

_____

31. stickleback   dog

flying fox   bat

blue-footed booby   fish

Manx   cat

muntjac   bird

whippet   deer

_____

_____

_____

_____

_____

_____

32. azure   pink

magenta   green

vermilion   brown

sienna   blue

olive   red

_____

_____

_____

_____

33. C   fist

      Au   weight

      Fe   digger

      Ag   sign

      Pb   copy

      Ne   lining

_____

_____

_____

_____

_____

_____

Periodic Table of the Elements

IA																	VIIA
H	IIA											IIIA	IVA	VA	VIA	VIIA	He
Li	Be											B	C	N	O	F	Ne
Na	Mg	IIIB	IVB	VB	VIB	VIIB	VIIIB			IB	IIB	Al	Si	P	S	Cl	Ar
K	Ca	Sc	Mn	Ti	V	Cr	Fe	Co	Ni	Cu	Zn	GA	Ge	As	Se	Br	Kr
Rb	Sr	Y	Te	Nb	Nb	Mo	Ru	Rh	Pd	Ag	Cd	In	Sn	Sb	Te	I	Xe
Cs	Ba	Lu	Hf	Ta	W	Re	Os	Ir	Pt	Au	Hg	Tl	Pb	Bi	Po	At	Rn
Fr	Ra	103 Lr	104	105	106												

34. patella   collarbone

larynx   shoulder blade

scapula   kneecap

clavicle   windpipe

trachea   voice box

_____

_____

_____

_____

_____

35. Eureka   Wyoming

Live Free or Die   Wisconsin

Industry   California

Forward   New Hampshire

Equal Rights   Utah

_____

_____

_____

_____

_____

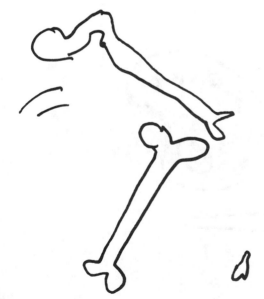

36. *Starry Night*   Mary

     My Mother   James

     American Gothic   Winslow

     Water Lilies   Grant

     Mother and Child   Vincent

     Sunlight on the Coast Claude

_____

_____

_____

_____

_____

_____

37. Barbera   Croatia

Merlot   Germany

Zinfandel   Italy

Concord   America

Riesling   France

_____

_____

_____

_____

_____

Find the Misfit

First find out what these things have in common, and then find the TWO misfits.

✳ answers on pages 363–368

I. 2 ¼ cups all-purpose flour

1 teaspoon baking soda

1 teaspoon salt

1 tablespoon olive oil

1 cup (2 sticks, ½ pound) butter, softened

¾ cup granulated (white) sugar

¾ cup packed brown sugar

1 teaspoon vanilla extract

2 eggs

2 cups (12-ounce package) chocolate chips

1 cup chopped nuts

1 cup raisins

_____

_____

2. Rat

Ox

Donkey

Tiger

Rabbit

Dragon

Snake

Horse

Goat

Monkey

Bear

Rooster

Dog

Pig

_____

_____

3. Alberta
British Columbia
Windsor
Manitoba
New Brunswick
Newfoundland and Labrador
Nova Scotia
Ontario
Victoria
Prince Edward Island
Quebec
Saskatchewan

_____

_____

4. rope
ice pick
lead pipe
revolver
wrench
chainsaw
candlestick
knife

_____

_____

5. Dizzy
   Charlie
   Miles
   Louis
   Chet
   Glenn
   Wynton

   _____

   _____

6. Dog
   Shoe
   Racecar
   Mouse
   Thimble
   Hat
   Wheelbarrow
   Cow

   _____

   _____

7. Hayes
Garfield
McKinley
Buchanan
Pierce
Franklin
Harding
Taft
Hamilton

8. Juneau
Denver
Augusta
Boston
Olympia
New York
Albuquerque

_____

_____

9. John
Paul
Mark
Matthew
George
Luke

_____

_____

10. *A Midsummer Night's Dream*
Canterbury Tales
Cymbeline
The Tempest
Twelfth Night
Titus Andronicus
Two Gentlemen of Verona
A Tale of Two Cities
Love's Labour's Lost
Othello

_____

_____

11. The Moon
    Jupiter
    Saturn
    Earth
    Pluto
    Mars
    Mercury

    _____

    _____

12. Poseidon

Ares

Aphrodite

Hades

Apollo

Zeus

Demeter

Hermes

Hephaestus

_____

_____

13. Giant slalom

      Figure skating

      Crew

      Ice hockey

      Ski jumping

      Biathlon

      Luge

      Curling

      Triathlon

_____

_____

14. Apricot

Ice

Bittersweet

Sea green

Brick red

Burnt sienna

Mud

Cornflower

Thistle

Salmon

Atomic tangerine

Timberwolf

Inchworm

_____

_____

15. Benin

Burkina Faso

Papua New Guinea

Gabon

Niger

Paraguay

Chad

Togo

_____

_____

16. Firefly
Spider
Butterfly
Cockroach
Mosquito
Dung beetle
Centipede
Termite
Ant
Dragonfly
Flea

_____

_____

17. *Forrest Gump*
    Mrs. Miniver
    West Side Story
    Chicago
    Terms of Endearment
    Gladiator
    Star Wars
    An American in Paris
    On the Waterfront
    The Sting
    The Color Purple

    _____

    _____

18. June 14

January 14

March 17

October 31

October 12

October 24

April 22

February 2

November 11

September 7

_____

_____

19. Oriole

Heron

Cardinal

Blue jay

Eagle

Hawk

Seagull

Falcon

Raven

Penguin

_____

_____

20. Abraham Lincoln

George Washington

Theodore Roosevelt

Benjamin Franklin

John Adams

Ulysses S. Grant

Andrew Jackson

William McKinley

Grover Cleveland

_____

_____

21. Oboe

Trombone

Bassoon

Clarinet

Saxophone

Harp

English horn

Bagpipes

_____

_____

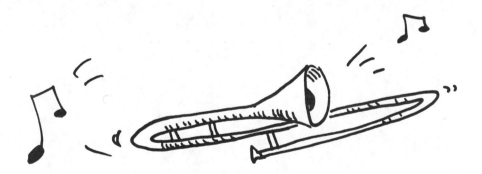

22. Zeus

Jupiter

Venus

Mars

Pluto

Mercury

Athena

Neptune

Juno

Diana

_____

_____

23. Salty Dog

Pink Lady

Hairy Navel

Cha Cha Cha

Sex on the Beach

Nixon

Royal Arrival

Flight to Mars

_____

_____

24. Bronco

Wrangler

Cowboy

Dakota

Yukon

Frontier

Tundra

Gold Rush

Explorer

_____

_____

25. Jaguar

Tapir

Toucan

Sloth

Macaw

Lion

Kinkajou

Porcupine

Boa constrictor

Morpho butterfly

Coatamundi

_____

_____

Memory Box #6

Want to blow the dust out of the old noggin? Trying to remember stuff and coming up dry? Well heat up your hippocampus with this sizzling hot visual puzzle and let the sun shine in again.

Take a close look at the images on this page. Give yourself a minute. Then, turn the page and see how many questions you can answer.

* answers on page 368

1. How many saguaro cacti were there?

   _____

2. Were there more black coyotes or white coyotes?

   _____

3. What kind of skulls were there—cattle or wolf?

   _____

4. How many armadillos were there?

   _____

5. How many birds were in the air?

   _____

6. Were they flying to the left or the right?

   _____

7. Was the lizard pointing up or down?

_____

8. How many coyotes were howling?

_____

9. Was it day or night?

_____

10. What two animals were peeking around the
cactus on the left side of the scene?

_____

Chapter Seven:

THAT'S
LOGICAL

We all get stuck in a rut as we cruise along in our busy lives. We get used to doing things and thinking about things in a specific way that works for us, and we travel the same old well-worn paths. That's fine for efficiency and when it comes to juggling schedules, meals, chores, and responsibilities, it's perect. But as we age our brains start to close off those paths less traveled and we start to lose functionality. So take those untread paths! Try these logic puzzles. These kinds of puzzles tap into your creative thought, ask you to think around a problem, and come up with new ways to see the familiar. They get you to tap into your problem-solving capabilities and sharpen the old wits. These puzzles require you to solve codes, untangle twisters, perform processes of elimination, and make use of your inner math skills. You'll feel the sparkle in your cerebrum before you can say "that's logical"!

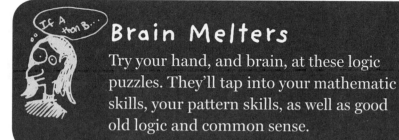

Brain Melters

Try your hand, and brain, at these logic puzzles. They'll tap into your mathematic skills, your pattern skills, as well as good old logic and common sense.

✳ answers on pages 369–372

I. Chip, Al, and Joe went clamming on the beach in Maine this summer. They gathered enough clams to fill a small crate. They went back to the campfire, washed the clams, and steamed them, then let them cool while they went swimming. Chip got out of the water first and secretly ate one-third of the clams while the others were still swimming. He ditched the shells in the woods and went back to the beach. While he and Joe were arguing over the biggest fish in the Atlantic, Al snuck off and decided to eat his third of the clams. He ate one-third of what was there. Al hid the shells, grabbed a beer, and went back to the beach. Then Joe took off to change out of his swim trunks. He decided to eat his third of the clams and ate one-third of what was left in the pot. He also hid the shells. None of the guys had a clue that the others had done the same thing. So when the sun set, they all gathered around the clams and divied up what was left in the pot. They each got 16.

How many clams were there to begin with?

_____

_____

_____

2. Helen was a lifelong hiker and was always on some trail. Last fall she took a walking tour of Italy. One day she was on a rural back road from Cortona to Perugia, and when she came to her trail junction, she discovered that the signpost had fallen down. The post was marked Perugia, Montepulciano, Umbertide, and Cortona. Helen was frustrated because she didn't know which trail to take and her family was expecting to meet her for dinner at a little vineyard in Perugia. She ended up making it in time to meet her family.

How did she get the sign in the right place and go in the right direction?

_____

_____

_____

3. There are *six countries* hidden in the text below. Can you find them all?

After a delicious lunch doused in chiles from Raj, a pan-Asian spot on the avenue, Vic had pains in his chest, chin, and throat that worried him. He decided to go to the emergency room. "Can a dash of hot sauce cause this amount of pain?" he screamed. "Watch your anger, man! You're going to work yourself into a hospital stay if you're not careful."

_____

_____

_____

_____

_____

_____

_____

4. If Ralph, the industrious robin, can find one worm in 15 minutes, and Rosie, the quick-on-her-feet robin, can find one worm every 12 minutes, and their chick, Rhonda, takes 20 minutes to eat a worm—and she eats all day long!—**how many worms will they have left at the end of a day?**

_____

5. Keith was excited about his first bake-off at the county fair. He was one of four pie makers who had won entry into the contest, and he was thrilled to show off his best apple pie. The contestants ranged in age from 14 to 22. There were two teenagers aged 14 and 17, and another contestant who had just turned 20. When ribbons were awarded, the contestant coming in last also happened to be the oldest contestant. Lynn was eight years older than the baker who came in second. Keith was neither the oldest nor the youngest, and Kai finished ahead of the 17-year old but didn't win. Leo, though his filling was delicious, had burned his crust a bit, and he didn't win either.

What was the ribbon order of pie makers?

_____

6. **Which of these words doesn't belong when shortened?**

    swish

    women

    shear

    glove

    seven

    brawl

    clover

    swing

    stone

7. **What is the name of this popular dog breed?**

A B

A B C D E F G H I J K L M N

A B C D E F G H I J K

A B C D E F G H I J K

A B C D E F G H

A B C D

_____

8. **Amy went to her daughter's swim meet and wrote down all the results. In the end, she was confused. Can you figure out from Amy's notes what the final results were?**

1. Peyton Poule beat Pat Paddler and Wanda Wader.
2. Sam Splash beat Wanda Wader, Pat Paddler, and Laneline Lena.
3. Goggles McCormick lost to Sam Splash.
4. J. B. Jammer beat Pat Paddler.
5. Goggles McCormick beat Chloe Chlorine.
6. J. B. Jammer lost to Chloe Chlorine and Sam Splash.
7. Pat Paddler beat Buck Brick.
8. Laneline Lena beat Goggles McCormick, Trenton Trout, and J. B. Jammer.
9. Trenton Trout lost to J. B. Jammer and Peyton Poule.
10. Buck Brick beat Trenton Trout.
11. Peyton Poule lost to Laneline Lena and Goggles McCormick.
12. Chloe Chlorine beat Pat Paddler, Peyton Poule, and Buck Brick.
13. Pat Paddler lost to Wanda Wader and Laneline Lena.
14. Wanda Wader beat J. B. Jammer and Buck Brick.

_____

_____

_____

9. Lydia's granddaughter, Greta, hid her precious pearl necklace. Greta, a precocious child of three, was happy to show off her shape-naming skills, deciding to make a game of the missing pearls. She told Lydia only one thing: "The necklace is inside a 6-inch-long cylinder surrounded by a thousand squares."

Where did Greta hide the necklace?

_____

10. Pete the pathologist had a petri dish in which he had collected a rare form of _Bacillus bunyonus_. The bacteria divide every minute in two equal parts that are the same size as the original organism. These then divide in the next minute, and so on. Pete's petri dish was full at noon.

At what time was Pete's petri dish half full?

_____

11. It's time for the Silver Fox Ballroom Dance competition.

Can you figure out which couple will win the highest score for this Freestyle Younameit Anythinggoes round?

* * * * *

The couples dancing were:

COUPLE #1 Ned and Ina Sneed III

COUPLE #2 Sam and Sue Sassfactor

COUPLE #3 Lyle and Lily Houndstooth

COUPLE #4 Chi-chi and Cha-cha Brown

COUPLE #5 Flame and Flora Freebird

* * * * *

Check out each couple's interview comments about their routine and then look at the Judges' Rules to see who earned the most points.

* * * * *

NED AND INA:

"After performing two whistle-flips, we did two elegant neck-knocks, a jaw-dropping sprawl-for-all and finished with a squeaking turnabout. As newcomers, we feel we did a pretty good job. We certainly had a lot of fun."

SAM AND SUE:

"We were happy with our shriek-twist and we're thrilled that we nailed the neck-knock before we had a sprawl-for-all. We worked super hard on our routine, and it showed."

LYLE AND LILY:

"After the two exhausting whistle-flips and the one flaming shriek-twist, we had a sassy sprawl-for-all and then finished it off with a flourishing shriek-twist in perfect tandem. We're really pleased."

CHI-CHI AND CHA-CHA:

"Ours was straightforward and classic: We did three harmonizing shriek-twists. I think the judges were impressed with our approach. We'll see if it pays off."

FLAME AND FLORA:

"People expected us to just go right in and do our signature neck-knocks, but we decided to stir things up a bit this time and toss in a heck of a squeaking turnabout followed by a surprising sprawl-for-all. It was bold, but so are we, dammit!"

✳ ✳ ✳ ✳

JUDGES' RULES

* Score three points for each whistle-flip, shriek-twist, or neck-knock
* Score ten points for each squeaking turnabout
* Divide the final score by two if you have a sprawl-for-all at any time.

_____

_____

_____

_____

12. It was a beautiful morning, and Dinah and all five of her best pals loaded into the minivan and headed out to hit the early yard sales. The first place they got to had a bunch of baseball cards, a broken toaster, some interesting clothes, and a few fishing rods. Nothing hugely exciting. The next place had a ton of old 8-track tapes and a working player to boot! Dinah and her pals cheered! They each dug through the baskets of tapes to grab the one they loved best.

In the end what they gathered was Led Zeppelin, Joan Baez, Dolly Parton, Patti Smith, ABBA, and Donny Osmond.

Using these clues, can you figure out who ended up with what?

* * * * *

Dinah chose an 8-track tape by Joan Baez. Lena hates pop and country music but got a tape she wanted. Kathy chose a solo singer and not Dolly Parton or Patti Smith. Mary chose a female singer. Liz chose a tape by a group. George chose ABBA.

_____

_____

_____

_____

_____

_____

13. How many 32-cent stamps are in a dozen?

_____

14. Things really heated up at the end of Tunetown's local music covers contest, and the audience got to vote for their favorite performance. Eunice's rendition of "Freebird" was not last—even though her performance was cut short when she twisted an ankle leaping from the stage into the arms of the audience. Madge only just managed to avoid last place, coming in third. The lady who rocked "Stayin' Alive" was very successful and took first place. Ida beat the woman who belted out "I Will Survive"—only because she was taken away for light-headedness due to low blood pressure; and the lady who sang "You Really Got Me" beat Vera.

Can you determine who sang what and who won?

_____

_____

_____

_____

15. It's Chip's birthday! When he adds 4 times his age 4 years from now to 5 times his age 5 years from now, he gets 10 times his current age.

How many candles will be on Chip's cake 3 years from now?

_____

16. How high would you have to count to get to the first number with an A in its spelling?

_____

17. Frankly, Frank was a flirt. He was in love with three women from his apartment complex, and couldn't decide which one to give his heart-shaped box of antioxidant-rich, extra-dark chocolate almond bark, so he decided to send each woman a Valentine's Day card.

In the end, Frank was burned, because each of the women thought the card came from someone else. He was left to munch on his heart-healthy treat all on his own.

From the following clues, can you work out the name of each woman, the color of each card Frank sent, and the name of the man each woman believed sent it?

＊ ＊ ＊ ＊ ＊

1. Unluckily for flirty Frank, when Miss Lulu Flaymon received her card, she thought it was from Brock.

2. When Miss Hortense Hubbahubba received her blue card, she told Miss Frieda Bellabella, and together they worked out that the card was from Dylan. It didn't occur to either of them that it was from flirty Frank!

3. The woman who received the red card was convinced it came from Ewan.

4. Neither Miss Frieda Bellabella nor Miss Hortense Hubbahubba received a pink card.

_____

_____

_____

18. Doug's apartment was quite the wildlife center. He had a number of parakeets, cats, and cockroaches in every nook and cranny. There were exactly 150 feet and 50 heads in total, not including Doug. There were twice as many cockroaches as cats.

How many of each animal were there?

_____

_____

_____

19. **Find a five-digit number that has no zeros in which no digit is repeated, where:**

   * The first digit is a prime number. (One is not a prime number.)
   * The second digit is the fifth digit minus the first digit.
   * The third digit is twice the first digit.
   * The fourth digit is the third digit plus three.
   * The fifth digit is the difference between the first digit and the fourth digit.

   _____

# # # # #

20. Recycler Renee really does her part for greening the world. On one of her highway hikes, she gathered forty-nine empty 1-liter plastic soda bottles. She knows it takes 6 ⅛ bottles to make a small fleece scarf.

At the end of the day how many small scarves will Renee be able to make?

_____

21. What runs but never walks,
Has a mouth and never talks,
Has a bed but never sleeps,
Has a body and never leaps?

_____

22. It was late and very dark outside when the woman who had been reading turned off the light and fell asleep. In the morning, she woke up refreshed. She wandered to the front porch and got the paper, brewed her coffee, and sipped it as she glanced at the headlines.

What she saw shocked her. The headline read:

SHIP WRECKS ON ROCKY COAST.
200 DEAD! ENTIRE STATE IN MOURNING.

The woman finished her coffee, got dressed, and called the police to turn herself in for the mass murder of 200 individuals.

Why?

_____

23. Biff made two elegant desserts for his fancy date with Ella that evening. Ella was sitting in the dining room while Biff went into the kitchen to serve the desserts. When he got there, he couldn't decide which of the two fancy desserts he should serve on which of the two plates.

How many choices did he have?

_____

24. Ella loved the chocolate decadence and yummy banana chiffon that Biff had made for her so much, she decided to have another date with him—even if he did take way too long in the kitchen between courses.

This date was a brunch, and Biff had a papaya and a mango, hoping to woo Ella with his knowledge of tropical fruit. This time, he had three fancy plates on which to display the fruit. And again, he was faced with too many choices. This time Biff asked Ella which fruit-plate combination she liked.

How many choices did they have?

_____

25. Take the number of days in a leap year, add the number of months with at least 30 days, divide by the unlucky number never represented in tall buildings, add the number of days in July, add the square root of nine, and divide by the number of days in a week.

Which month does the number you're left with represent?

_____

Phoning It In

Stand-Up Stan works at the phone company. He thinks he really knocks 'em dead at the switchboard, but everyone wants him to hang it up. His material is ancient—prehistoric, really. Before his routine he gets a mysterious phone call giving him a joke and a code for the punch line.

✳ answers on page 373

Using a phone pad as a decoder, can you figure out Stan's routine?

1. What made the dinosaurs extinct?

8-4-3-9   6-3-8-3-7   8-6-6-5   2-2-8-4-7!

_____

2. What's a dinosaur's favorite flooring material?

7-3-7-8-4-5-3-7!

_____

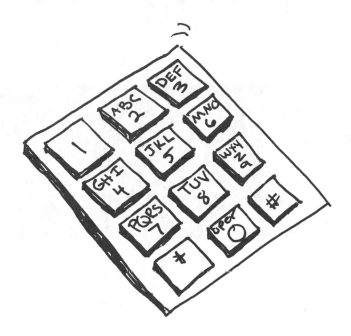

3. Why did the triceratops eat the steel factory?

7-4-3   9-2-7   2   7-5-2-6-8   3-2-8-3-7!

_____

4. What did the T. rex tell the doctor after he
stubbed his toe?

4-8-'-7   3-4-6-6-7-6-7-3!

_____

5. What do you give a nauseated dinosaur?

7-5-3-6-8-9   6-3   7-6-6-6!

_____

Behind the Eight Ball

Eight-Ball Edna is having a bad day. She had several messages from the underworld, but they were all in code. Lucky for Edna, she had a Magic 8 Ball, which gave her this clue.

✳ answers on pages 373–374

What were Edna's otherworldly messages?

1. Her horoscope said:
   Hsq sllwflagf lg lzw kayfk!

   _____

2. Her fortune cookie said:
   Egfwq oadd ugew qgmj osq lgvsq.

   _____

3. A psychic stopped her on the street and said:
   Qgm oadd tw jauz!

   _____

4. The Ouija Board said:

Lgvsq ak qgmj dmucq vsq.

_____

5. And her clairvoyant grandson said:

Tmq s dgllwjq laucwl!

_____

Morse Code

Rocky was serving time for bad jokes. He'd been put away for gagging his audience and leaving them in stitches. He says he's an innocent guy—just a victim of bad humor. You be the judge. Rocky now does his routine by clunking his head on the wall in Morse Code so all the other convicts can hear him.

✳ answers on page 374

Can you figure out his jokes?

1. The robber's defense was based on poison ivy. Why?

     ·—· ·— ··· ····

     —·· · —·—· ·· ··· ·· ——— —· ···

     _____

     _____

2. How come the blanket thief was never prosecuted?

_ .... . .-. .

.-- .- ... .- -.-. .. --. -.-. --- .... . .-. .-- .-

_____

_____

3. How did the shampoo thief escape?

.... . -- .- -.. . .- -.-. .-.. . .- -.

-- . _ .- .-- .- -.-

_____

_____

4. What happened to the guy at the coffee stand?

.... . -.. --- - -- .-- -.. --. . -..

_____

_____

5. How did the pork-industry crime ring
get busted?

... --- -- . --- -.. . ... -.-. .-- . .- .-.. . -..

_____

_____

BUSTED!

The bust of Benson Bassoonblaur is bent out of shape. He feels the classics are being neglected. Can you figure out which of these classic composers Benson most admires?

✳ answers on page 375

∽ CODE ∾

a = ♋	j = *ℰ*	s = ♦
b = ♌	k = &	t = ◆
c = ♍	l = ●	u = ◆
d = ♎	m = ○	v = ❖
e = ♏	n = ■	w = ◆
f = ♐	o = ☐	x = ☒
g = ♑	p = ◻	y = ◹
h = ♒	q = ◻	z = ⌘
i = ♓	r = ◻	

1. ♌ ♍ ♏ ♦ ♒ ☐ ❖ ♏ ■

_____

2. ♌ ☐ ♋ ♒ ◯ ♦

_____

3. ◆ ♍ ♒ ♋ ♓ & □ ❖ ◆ & ⬠

_____

4. ♍ ♒ □ □ ♓ ■

_____

5. ◆ ♍ ♒ ◆ ♌ ♏ □ ◆

_____

6. ♍ □ □ ● ♋ ■ ♎

_____

7. ● ♓ ◆ ⌘ ◆

_____

8. □ □ □ & □ ♐ ♓ ♏ ❖

_____

9. ♒ ♋ ⬠ ♎ ■

_____

10. ♌ ♋ ♍ ♒

_____

Memory Box #7

Uncle who? And which cousin is it that walks tightropes? Feeling like a filial failure at family reunions? Get the familiar back into family with this fun visual memory puzzle.

Take a close look at the images on this page. Give yourself a minute. Then, turn the page and see how many questions you can answer.

✱ answers on page 375

1. How many female relatives were pictured?

   _____

2. Who was next to Uncle Ned?

   _____

3. What animal was with Grandpa Keith?

   _____

4. Was Kolya above the giraffe or beside it?

   _____

5. What was Myrtle?

   _____

6. Were Maura and Ted below Cindy or Amy?

   _____

7. Who had curly hair?

_____

8. Who wore an eye patch?

_____

9. Who was wearing a hat?

_____

10. What was Mama Lena doing?

_____

CHAPTER ONE
WHAT WAS THAT WORD AGAIN?

WORDS—DEFINITIONS ANSWERS
pages 19–28

1-B	10-B	19-B
2-A	11-A	20-C
3-C	12-C	21-A
4-C	13-B	22-B
5-B	14-C	23-C
6-A	15-A	24-B
7-B	16-A	25-A
8-C	17-B	
9-A	18-A	

HINK-PINK ANSWERS
pages 29–37

1. Drab crab
2. Lobster mobster
3. Wiccan chicken
4. Poi boy
5. Shade maid
6. Merino bambino
7. Cough-off
8. Roach coach
9. Fertile turtle
10. Glam cam
11. Balmy mommy
12. Poster roaster
13. Canned band

14. Green sheen
15. Muzzle nuzzle
16. Phone tone
17. Glad dad
18. Groomer rumor
19. Sleepy tipi
20. Shady lady
21. Butter cutter
22. Smart art
23. Stick trick
24. Loose goose
25. Singer zinger

HOMOPHONES ANSWERS

pages 38–45

1. ad/add
2. ail/ale
3. flour/flower
4. friar/fryer
5. pore/pour
6. pi/pie
7. peace/piece
8. all/awl
9. wrap/rap
10. beau/bow
11. role/roll
12. nit/knit
13. blew/blue
14. hail/hale
15. hear/here
16. some/sum
17. higher/hire
18. sleigh/slay
19. beet/beat
20. ring/wring
21. knows/nose
22. bazaar/bizarre
23. in/inn
24. made/maid
25. moan/mown

MEMORY BOX #1 ANSWERS

pages 46–49

I. three; **2.** October 9; **3.** male; **4.** six; **5.** four; **6.** half-full;
7. Seattle; **8.** no (it's off the hook); **9.** April; **10.** two

CHAPTER TWO
WHO WAS THAT?

SING IT! ANSWERS

pages 53–60

I. "50 Ways to Leave Your Lover," Paul Simon

2. The desert; "A Horse with No Name," America

3. "Last Train to Clarksville," The Monkees

4. "The Sound of Silence," Simon and Garfunkel

5. "Rock Lobster," "Private Idaho," and "Love Shack," B-52's

6. "The Circle Game," Joni Mitchell

7. "Burning Down the House" and "Take Me to the River," Talking Heads

8. "Don't Stop," Fleetwood Mac

9. "Shock the Monkey," Peter Gabriel

10. "Up on the Roof," "Walking Man," and "Steamroller," James Taylor

11. "Blue Hawaii" and "Blue Suede Shoes," Elvis Presley

12. "Paint It Black," The Rolling Stones

13. Bachman-Turner Overdrive and "You Ain't Seen Nothin' Yet"

14. "Bennie and the Jets," Elton John

15. "Stairway to Heaven," Led Zeppelin

16. "Sweet Home Alabama," Lynyrd Skynyrd

17. "What's New, Pussycat?," Tom Jones

18. Bobby "Boris" Pickett and the Crypt-Kickers

19. "Son of a Preacher Man," Dusty Springfield

20. Gordon Sumner (Sting), Andy Summers, and Stewart Copeland. "Roxanne" (April 1978) was their first hit.

21. "Video Killed the Radio Star," The Buggles

22. Mick Jagger

23. The band members' first names: Agnetha, Benny, Björn, and Anni-Frid

24. "Summer Breeze," Seals and Crofts

25. Steely Dan

I THINK I SAW THIS ONE ALREADY ANSWERS
pages 61–75

1. "One thing I can't stand . . . " is a line from another Humphrey Bogart movie, *Key Largo*.

2. JERRY LEWIS was not a member of the rat pack.

3. THEY'VE ALL DIRECTED FILMS IN WHICH THEY HAVE ALSO PERFORMED. Allen and *Annie Hall* (1977); Beatty and *Reds* (1981); Clooney and *Good Night, and Good Luck* (2005); Eastwood and *Million Dollar Baby* (2004); Gibson and *Braveheart* (1995); Kelly and *Singin' in the Rain* (1952).

4. **1**-E, **2**-B, **3**-A, **4**-F, **5**-C, **6**-D

5. ALFRED HITCHCOCK. Hitchcock made it a game for film audiences to spot him, usually as a passerby in the background of a scene. For example, in *Lifeboat*, set in a small boat adrift at sea, he showed up in before-and-after photos in a newspaper diet ad.

6. SEAN PENN has not yet done Shakespeare in the movies, but all the other actors have: Gibson in *Hamlet*; Kline in *A Midsummer Night's Dream*; Pacino in *The Merchant of Venice*; Washington in *Much Ado About Nothing*; Welles in *Macbeth* and *The Tragedy of Othello*.

7. JOEY BISHOP sat in for Carson a total of 177 times; JOAN RIVERS came in second at 93 times.

8. **1**-E, **2**-A, **3**-F, **4**-D, **5**-G, **6**-B, **7**-C

9. CARY GRANT and KEVIN KLINE

10. Burghoff played the company clerk, CPL. WALTER "RADAR" O'REILLY.

11. KATHARINE HEPBURN won four Oscars for *Morning Glory* (1933); *Guess Who's Coming to Dinner* (1967); *The Lion in Winter* (1968); and *On Golden Pond* (1981). The others on the list won fewer Oscars.

12. HUGH GRANT

13. JOHN, WALTER, and ANJELICA HUSTON

14. *TITANIC* earned a record 14 nominations and picked up 11 Academy Awards.

15. MEG RYAN, who starred with Cage in *City of Angels* (1998); Crowe in *Proof of Life* (2000); Crystal in *When Harry Met Sally* (1989); Hanks in *Sleepless in Seattle* (1993) (and other films); Kline in *French Kiss* (1995); and Jackman in *Kate and Leopold* (2001).

16. They all won Academy Awards for Best Picture. Only four other musicals qualified for that honor: *The Broadway Melody* (1929); *An American in Paris* (1951); *Gigi* (1958); and *Chicago* (2002).

17. RON HOWARD, who starred as Opie Taylor on *The Andy Griffith Show* in the 1960s and as Richie Cunningham on *Happy Days* in the 1970s and 1980s. His movie directorial talent has covered both comedy and drama, ranging from *Splash* (1984) to *The Da Vinci Code* (2006).

18. They were all members of the cast of TV's *Saturday Night Live*.

19. RYAN and TATUM O'NEAL in *Paper Moon* (1973); HENRY and JANE FONDA in *On Golden Pond* (1981); MARTIN and CHARLIE SHEEN in *Wall Street* (1987); KIRK and MICHAEL DOUGLAS in *It Runs in the Family* (2003); WILL and JADEN SMITH in *The Pursuit of*

Happyness (2006); and JERRY and BEN STILLER in
The Heartbreak Kid (2007).

20. EBENEZER SCROOGE

21. *A HARD DAY'S NIGHT*

22. They all portrayed the comic-book hero BATMAN in
the movies: West in 1966; Keaton in 1989 and 1992;
Kilmer in 1995, Clooney in 1997; and Bale in 2005
and 2008.

23. STEPHEN KING

24. 1-F, 2-D, 3-B, 4-A, 5-C, 6-E

25. BOB HOPE hosted the Oscars a record 18 times.
His nearest competitor was Billy Crystal with 8 times.
Nobody else has come close.

BOOKWORM ANSWERS:
pages 76–92

1. 1-B, 2-C, 3-E, 4-A, 5-D

2. 1-C, 2-A, 3-E, 4-B, 5-D

3. JOHN F. KENNEDY was awarded a Pulitzer in 1957 for
Profiles in Courage.

4. STEPHEN KING. Without even counting sequels or films derived from short stories, upwards of two dozen King novels have found their way onto the silver screen.

5. DOROTHY PARKER. The essayist and poet stuck to witty verse, acerbic reviews, and caustic commentary on her times, especially the 1920s and 1930s.

6. Each was derived from lines in Shakespearean plays.

7. GERTRUDE STEIN. Toklas was her longtime secretary and life partner.

8. 1-B, 2-D, 3-E, 4-C, 5-A

9. PHYLLIS WHEATLEY—The one-time slave's book, *Poems on Various Subjects*, was published in 1773, three years before the U.S. Declaration of Independence. The others are twentieth-century writers.

10. WILLIAM STYRON, who wrote *The Confessions of Nat Turner*, a fictional account of an actual slave revolt, was himself a descendant of Southern slave owners.

11. J. K. ROWLING, whose decade-long run of bestsellers ended following the seventh and supposedly final book in the Harry Potter series.

12. **1-**"E. L." for Edgar Lawrence

    2-"F." for Francis

    3-"H. L." for Henry Louis

    4-"J.R.R." for John Ronald Reuel

    5-"E. B." for Elwyn Brooks

13. THE HOLY BIBLE. In its various forms, the Bible has sold more than six billion copies worldwide since it was first published in the fifteenth century.

14. *ULYSSES* was No.1 and *A PORTRAIT OF THE ARTIST AS A YOUNG MAN* was No. 3. (These books were separated by Fitzgerald's *The Great Gatsby* in the No. 2 spot.)

15. **1-** *MOBY-DICK* (Herman Melville)
    2-*1984* (George Orwell)
    3-*DON QUIXOTE* (Miguel de Cervantes)
    4-*FAHRENHEIT 451* (Ray Bradbury)
    5-*THE CATCHER IN THE RYE* (J. D. Salinger)

16. *BILLY BUDD,* by Herman Melville (published posthumously in 1924)

17. **1-**E, **2-**F, **3-**C, **4-**B, **5-**A, **6-**D

18. *TARZAN* (He was introduced in the 1914 novel *Tarzan of the Apes* by Edgar Rice Burroughs, who went on to write twenty-three sequels. The character first appeared in comic-strip form in 1929.)

19. 1-D, 2-F, 3-E, 4-B, 5-A, 6-C

20. HERCULE POIROT, the Belgian detective invented in 1920 by British author Agatha Christie, who died five months after the *Times* noted the passing of her famous fictional creation.

21. PHILIP MARLOWE was played by Bogart in *The Big Sleep*, Gould in *The Long Goodbye*, Mitchum in *Farewell* and *My Lovely*, Montgomery in *Lady in the Lake*, and Powell in *Murder, My Sweet*.

22. 1-C, 2-E, 3-A, 4-B, 5-F, 6-D

23. HOLMES himself was the first-person narrator of "The Adventure of the Blanched Soldier" and "The Adventure of the Lion's Mane" in *The Case Book of Sherlock Holmes.*

24. They were PIGS, dominated by the evil Napoleon, a Berkshire boar.

25. 1-C, 2-D, 3-E, 4-B, 5-A

HISTORY TRIVIA ANSWERS

pages 93–103

1. EIGHTY-SEVEN (a score is twenty)

2. EACH NAME WAS SHARED BY TWO PRESIDENTS
   (John and John Quincy Adams; Andrew and Lyndon
   Johnson; William and Benjamin Harrison; Theodore and
   Franklin Roosevelt; George H. W. and George W. Bush)

3. GERALD R. FORD (confirmed by Congress as Republican
   vice president when Spiro Agnew resigned in 1973, he
   succeeded to the presidency a year later when Richard
   Nixon resigned. Ford ran for President on his own in 1976
   but lost to Democrat Jimmy Carter)

4. MEMPHIS, TENNESSEE (where he had gone to support
   a strike by public sanitation workers)

5. "WE THE PEOPLE . . . "

6. SANDRA DAY O'CONNOR

7. ALASKA (January 3, 1959) and HAWAII (August 21, 1959)

8. GEN. DWIGHT D. EISENHOWER

9. ALAN SHEPARD (who piloted *Freedom 7* on a
   fifteen-minute suborbital flight on May 5, 1961)

10. JEFFERSON DAVIS (former member of Congress and U.S. secretary of war)

11. IRAN, IRAQ, NORTH KOREA

12. LOUIS XIV of France, and ELIZABETH I of England (the "Virgin Queen")

13. 1-C, 2-D, 3-A, 4-F, 5-B, 6-E

14. KATRINA

15. WOODROW WILSON, CALVIN COOLIDGE, HERBERT HOOVER, RONALD REAGAN

16. *THE SPIRIT OF ST. LOUIS*

17. OHIO

18. FRANKLIN ROOSEVELT (who was subsequently elected to a fourth term but died shortly after his inauguration)

19. LEAGUE OF NATIONS (Headquartered in Geneva, the league was weakened at the outset because Germany and Russia were barred from joining and the United States refused to join)

20. BILL OF RIGHTS

21. 1-F, 2-J, 3-E, 4-H, **5**-A, **6**-C, **7**-B, 8-I, **9**-G, **10**-D

22. KITTY HAWK, NORTH CAROLINA

23. ANDREW JOHNSON in 1868; BILL CLINTON in 1999 (Impeachment proceedings were begun against Richard Nixon in 1974, but he resigned before they could be completed)

24. WORLD TRADE CENTER In New York City and THE PENTAGON outside Washington, D.C.

25.

NEW HAMPSHIRE	DELAWARE
MASSACHUSETTS	MARYLAND
CONNECTICUT	VIRGINIA
RHODE ISLAND	NORTH CAROLINA
NEW YORK	SOUTH CAROLINA
NEW JERSEY	GEORGIA
PENNSYLVANIA	

MEMORY BOX #2 ANSWERS
pages 104–107

1. left; **2.** one; **3.** one (the other is a snorkeler);
4. clam; **5.** thirteen; **6.** afternoon; **7.** west; **8.** one;
9. dark; **10.** hammerhead

CHAPTER THREE
WHAT WAS THAT, AGAIN?

IN OTHER WORDS ANSWERS
pages 111–121

1. A penny for your thoughts.

2. His bark is worse than his bite.

3. The ball is in your court.

4. Let's cross that bridge when we come to it.
   Don't burn your bridges.

5. A man's home is his castle.

6. Counting your chickens before they hatch.

7. A bird in the hand is worth two in the bush.
   Birds of a feather flock together.

8. Don't look a gift horse in the mouth.

9. Keep your fingers crossed.
   Don't cut off your nose to spite your face.

10. It is better to have loved and lost than never
    to have loved at all.

11. It takes two to tango.

12. Love is blind.

13. Rain, rain go away. Come again some other day.

14. Silence is golden.

15. The walls have ears.

16. Fight fire with fire.

17. There's a light at the end of the tunnel.
The lights are on but nobody's home.

18. No pain, no gain.
If at first you don't succeed, try, try again.

19. Once in a blue moon.
'Til the cows come home.

20. If you can't stand the heat, then get out of the kitchen.

21. Time flies.

22. Money talks.

23. Skeleton in the closet.

24. Blood is thicker than water.

25. What do you do with a drunken sailor?
Dead men tell no tales.

SCRAMBLERS ANSWERS

pages 122–131

1. "Brevity is the soul of lingerie." DOROTHY PARKER

2. "She got her good looks from her father. He's a plastic surgeon." GROUCHO MARX

3. "Virtue has never been as respectable as money." MARK TWAIN

4. "She developed a persistent troubled frown which gave her the expression of someone who is trying to repair a watch with his gloves on." JAMES THURBER

5. "It's not that I'm afraid to die. I just don't want to be there when it happens." WOODY ALLEN

6. "Hanging is too good for a man who makes puns. He should be drawn and quoted." FRED ALLEN

7. "The only thing worse than being talked about is not being talked about." OSCAR WILDE

8. "I grew up to have my father's looks, my father's speech patterns, my father's posture, my father's walk, my father's opinions and my mother's contempt for my father." JULES FEIFFER

9. "We learn from experience that men never learn anything from experience." GEORGE BERNARD SHAW

10. "I like children. If they're properly cooked." W. C. FIELDS

11. "Yesterday I was a dog. Today I'm a dog. Tomorrow I'll probably still be a dog. Sigh! There's so little hope for advancement." SNOOPY (CHARLES SCHULZ)

12. "It is easy to be brave from a safe distance." AESOP

13. "Early to bed and early to rise makes a man healthy, wealthy, and wise." BENJAMIN FRANKLIN

14. "I think we agree, the past is over." GEORGE W. BUSH

15. "Accidents will occur in the best regulated families." CHARLES DICKENS

16. "By nature, men are nearly alike; by practice, they get to be wide apart." CONFUCIUS

17. "Be careful about reading health books. You may die of a misprint." MARK TWAIN

18. "Assume a virtue, if you have it not." WILLIAM SHAKESPEARE

19. "A lifetime of happiness! No man alive could bear it; it would be hell on earth." GEORGE BERNARD SHAW

20. "Even if you're on the right track, you'll get run over if you just sit there." WILL ROGERS

21. "Go, and never darken my towels again." GROUCHO MARX

22. "A woman is like a tea bag—you never know how strong she is until she gets in hot water." ELEANOR ROOSEVELT

23. "I cannot live without books." THOMAS JEFFERSON

24. "In wildness is the preservation of the world." HENRY DAVID THOREAU

25. "I hate quotations. Tell me what you know." RALPH WALDO EMERSON

FIND THE MISSPELLED WORD ANSWERS
pages 132–139

1. AMATEUR

2. PRINCIPLE

3. VACUUM

4. CEMETERY

5. INADVERTENT

6. RESTAURANT

7. PASTIME

8. MISSPELLED

9. RECEIVED

10. HEIGHT

11. PLAYWRIGHT

12. PURSUE

13. ECSTASY

14. FORTY

15. MATHEMATICS

16. RASPBERRIES

17. SORCERERS

18. SOUVENIR

19. PARALLEL

20. FIERY

21. SEIZE

22. PLAGIARISM

23. ANOINTED

24. PROCEED

25. LEISURELY

MEMORY BOX #3 ANSWERS
pages 140–143

1. Ugh, Ow, and Oof; 2. Upper Migraine; 3. Upper Migraine, Lower Migraine, Bumknee, and Aykee; 4. Lower Migraine; 5. Napz; 6. Huh and Grayur; 7. Grayur; 8. Ow; 9. Driskin; 10. Upper Migraine

CHAPTER FOUR
WORD SURGERY

WORD TRANSFORMERS ANSWERS
pages 147–158

1. TIE
   PIE
   PIG
   PEG
   LEG

2. HEAD
   BEAD
   BEAT
   BOAT
   BOOT
   FOOT

3. GIFT
   LIFT
   LIFE
   LIVE
   LOVE

4. WET
   PET
   PAT
   PAY
   PRY
   DRY

5. OLD
   ODD
   ADD
   AID
   HID
   HIP
   HEP
   HEW
   NEW

6. BOOM
   ROOM
   ROAM
   REAM
   REAR
   HEAR

7. HARD
   CARD
   CART
   CAST
   EAST
   EASY

8. NORTH
   FORTH
   FORTS
   SORTS
   SOOTS
   SOOTH
   SOUTH

9. ARM
   ARE
   AYE
   LYE
   LEE
   LEG

10. SLEEP
    BLEEP
    BLEED
    BREED
    BREAD
    DREAD
    DREAM

11. TOP
    TON
    SON
    SUN
    GUN

12. HOT
    HIT
    HIP
    LIP

13. HIP
    HOP
    HOG
    JOG

14. ARE
    APE
    APT
    OPT
    OUT

15. CAT
    COT
    COG
    DOG

16. HOT
    HOE
    TOE
    TON
    SON
    SUN
    NUN

17. STARE
    STARS
    SEARS
    TEARS

18. FIRE
FORE
FORT
FOOT
FOOL
FOUL

19. PAWN
PAWS
PEWS
PENS
PINS
PING
KING

20. BLURT
BLURS
SLURS
SPURS
SPARS
SPARE
SHARE

21. SEED
SLED
SLEW
SLOW
GLOW
GROW

22. GREEN
GREED
TREED
TREES
TRESS
CRESS
CRASS
GRASS

23. TREE
FREE
FRET
FEET
FELT
FELL
FALL

24. COOK
HOOK
HOOD
FOOD

25. WARM
WORM
FORM
FORD
FOLD
COLD

SHRINKY-THINKS ANSWERS
pages 159–165

1. BUSH/BUS
2. TIGER/TIER
3. SUPPER/SUPER
4. FEATHER/FATHER
5. TETHER/ETHER
6. STUNG/SUNG
7. KING/KIN
8. PRETTY/PETTY
9. PARIS/PARS
10. PEDALED/PEALED
11. TONGUE/TOGUE
12. BRAIN/BRAN
13. THRILL/TRILL
14. SMELL/SELL
15. BREAD/READ
16. FOURTH/FORTH
17. PRESENT/RESENT
18. PILOT/PLOT
19. CRASH/CASH
20. PENDANT/PEDANT
21. PRUNE/RUNE
22. SIMILE/SMILE
23. TWIG/WIG
24. SAGA/SAG
25. MOUSE/MUSE

LOP THE TOP ANSWERS

pages 166–173

1. STEAL/TEAL
2. SHEAR/HEAR
3. BLOW/LOW
4. SWISH/WISH
5. WOMEN/OMEN
6. GLOVE/LOVE
7. FLOWER/LOWER
8. BREAD/READ
9. MEAT/EAT
10. GRAM/RAM
11. CREAM/REAM
12. WHIM/HIM
13. MARK/ARK

14. STALL/TALL
15. SHOVEL/HOVEL
16. AMAZE/MAZE
17. SHOE/HOE
18. WHEAT/HEAT
19. TRACK/RACK
20. GRAVE/RAVE
21. BLOOM/LOOM
22. THICK/HICK
23. SOAK/OAK
24. WALL/ALL
25. FRAY/RAY

MEMORY BOX #4 ANSWERS

pages 174–177

1. eighteen; **2.** *You Can Help!*; **3.** Wayne Dwops; **4.** *Tight Squeeze*; **5.** Lynn O'Liam; **6.** *Fake It!*; **7.** Arthur Itis; **8.** A. King; **9.** Ann Thrax; **10.** *Neither a Borrower*

CHAPTER FIVE
THAT'S A DIFFERENT WAY TO LOOK AT IT

ANAGRAMS ANSWERS

pages 181–191

Athletes

1. Muhammad Ali
2. Babe Ruth
3. Tiger Woods
4. Michael Jordan
5. O. J. Simpson

Political Figures

1. Hillary Clinton
2. George Bush
3. Dick Cheney
4. Jimmy Carter
5. Nancy Pelosi

Actors

1. George Clooney
2. Mel Gibson
3. Clint Eastwood
4. Eddie Murphy
5. Meg Ryan

Singers

1. David Bowie
2. Elvis Presley
3. Madonna
4. Michael Jackson
5. Mick Jagger

Authors

1. Ernest Hemingway
2. Mark Twain
3. John Grisham
4. Norman Mailer
5. Tom Wolfe

Comedians

1. David Letterman
2. Robin Williams
3. Bob Hope
4. Steve Martin
5. Bill Murray

Historical Figures

1. Robert E. Lee
2. Richard Nixon
3. Napoleon
4. Christopher Columbus
5. Eleanor Roosevelt

Composer-Songwriters

1. Paul McCartney
2. Aaron Copeland
3. Gershwin
4. Bob Dylan
5. Cole Porter

Artists

1. Pablo Picasso
2. Norman Rockwell
3. Leonardo da Vinci
4. Andrew Wyeth
5. Toulouse-Lautrec

Foreign Leaders

1. Fidel Castro
2. Queen Elizabeth
3. Saddam Hussein
4. Adolf Hitler
5. Boris Yeltsin

REBUSES ANSWERS
pages 192–198

1. crab cakes
2. Bloody Mary
3. hot fudge sundae
4. *Cat on a Hot Tin Roof*
5. *Catcher in the Rye*
6. New York minute
7. b-eam me up, Scotty!
8. stifle yourself
9. Yabba Dabba DOO
10. twilight zone
11. I'm no crook
12. dynomite
13. where's the beef?
14. *The Love Boat*
15. baby boomer
16. *Yankee Doodle Dandy*
17. T-bird
18. sock hop
19. all's well that ends well
20. nice to meet you

WORD PICTURES ANSWERS

pages 199–204

1. I understand
2. space invaders
3. forgive and forget
4. red in the face
5. trail mix
6. no one to blame
7. all mixed up
8. paradox
9. tuna fish
10. one thing after another
11. history repeats itself
12. one in a million
13. but on second thought

14. hard up
15. head over heels
16. in between jobs
17. growing economy
18. try to understand
19. a walk in the park
20. point blank
21. you're under arrest
22. right beside me
23. double take
24. time after time
25. big bird

PICTURE THIS ANSWERS

pages 205–211

1. watchdog
2. shutterbug
3. boxing match
4. deviled egg
5. bookworm
6. mailman
7. butterfly
8. fan club
9. milk shake
10. home run

11. fruit bowl
12. catfish
13. basketball
14. pancake
15. horseshoe crab
16. football
17. eyeball
18. flower bulb
19. wisdom tooth
20. firecracker

MEMORY BOX #5 ANSWERS

pages 212–215

1. twenty-seven; 2. striped (seven); 3. three; 4. yes; 5. nine;
6. to the left (seven); 7. three; 8. striped; 9. no; 10. six

CHAPTER SIX
WHAT DO YOU KNOW?

MIX UP MATCH ANSWERS
pages 219–247

1. These are television shows and the cities they are based in.

    Grey's Anatomy—Seattle

    WKRP—Cincinnati

    Cheers—Boston

    Friends—New York

    All in the Family—Queens

    Laverne & Shirley—Milwaukee

2. These are scientific classification words and the contemporary characters that they describe.

    porcine (pig)—Porky

    equine (horse)—Mr. Ed

    canine (dog)—Pluto

    feline (cat)—Felix

3. These are playing cards that are part of well-known names.

King Tut

Queen Latifah

Jack London

Ace Ventura

Deuce Bigalow

4. These are famous advertising slogans and their companies.

"Can you hear me now?"—Verizon

"I'm lovin' it!"—McDonalds

"Love the skin you're in."—Dove

"My life. My card."—American Express

"It's the real thing."—Coca-Cola

5. These are scientific classification words and the contemporary characters that they describe.

porifera (sponge)—SpongeBob SquarePants

hominid (human)—The Simpsons

ungulate (hoofed mammal)—Rudolph the
        Red-Nosed Reindeer

arachnid (spider)—Charlotte

rodent (small furry animal)—Mickey Mouse

6. These are famous characters and the novels from which they come.

    Catherine—*Wuthering Heights*
    Isabel—*Portrait of a Lady*
    Nick—*The Great Gatsby*
    Tom—*The Grapes of Wrath*
    Santiago—*The Old Man and the Sea*
    Florentino—*Love in the Time of Cholera*

7. These are the characters in the TV sitcom *The Munsters* and the things that they represent.

    Grandpa—Vampire
    Herman—Frankenstein's monster
    Eddie—Werewolf
    Spot—Fire-breathing dragon
    Marilyn—Blonde

8. These are famous characters and what animals they are.

      Wilbur—pig (*Charlotte's Web*)

      Buck—dog (*Call of the Wild*)

      Mickey—mouse (Disney's Mickey Mouse)

      Kermit—frog (Muppets' Kermit the Frog)

      George—monkey (*Curious George*)

      Misty—pony (*Misty of Chincoteague*)

      Peter—rabbit (*The Tale of Peter Rabbit*)

9. These are famous characters and the novels from which they come.

      Holden—*The Catcher in the Rye*

      Pip—*Great Expectations*

      Scarlett—*Gone with the Wind*

      Scout—*To Kill a Mockingbird*

      Selden—*The House of Mirth*

10. These are famous characters and the novels from which they come.

    Jo—*Little Women*

    Hester—*The Scarlet Letter*

    Jim—*Treasure Island*

    Laura—*Little House on the Prairie*

    Ebenezer—*A Christmas Carol*

11. These are famous character pairs in television sitcoms.

    Jerry and Elaine (*Seinfeld*)

    Hawkeye and Hot Lips (*M*A*S*H*)

    Chandler and Monica (*Friends*)

    Niles and Maris (*Frasier*)

    Tabitha and Darrin (*Bewitched*)

12. These are current and former names of African countries.

    Democratic Republic of Congo: Zaire

    Benin: Dahomey

    Burkina Faso: Upper Volta

    Lesotho: Basutoland

    Botswana: Bechuanaland

    Zimbabwe: Rhodesia

13. These are comic strips and their creators.

    Fred Basset—Alex Graham

    Garfield—Jim Davis

    Dilbert—Scott Adams

    Blondie—Chic and Dean Young

    Calvin and Hobbes—Bill Watterson

14. These are famous celebrity couples.

    Tom Cruise and Katie Holmes

    Brad Pitt and Angelina Jolie

    Desi Arnaz and Lucille Ball

    Humphrey Bogart and Lauren Bacall

    Katharine Hepburn and Spencer Tracy

15. These are cartoonists and their comic strips.

    Reg Smythe—*Andy Capp*

    Bob Montana—*Archie*

    Johnny Hart—*B.C.*

    Chester Gould—*Dick Tracy*

    Charles Schulz—*Peanuts*

16. These are *Saturday Night Live* performers and their characters' famous one-liners.

    Gilda Radner, Miss Emily Litella, "Never mind."

    Eddie Murphy, Gumby, "I'm Gumby dammit!"

    Billy Crystal, Fernando, "It's better to look fabulous than to feel fabulous."

    Dana Carvey, Church Lady, "Isn't that special?"

    Mike Myers, Deiter, "Now is the time on Sprockets vhen ve dance!"

    Dan Akroyd, "Jane, you ignorant slut."

17. These are *Saturday Night Live* performers and their characters' famous one-liners.

    Mike Myers, Linda Richman, "I'm a little *verklempt*."

    Chris Farley, Matt Foley, "You could be living in a van, down by the river."

    David Spade, Flight Attendant, "Buh BYE!"

    Jon Lovitz, Master Thespian, "Acting!"

    John Belushi, Pete, from the Olympia Café, "Cheeburger, cheeburger, cheeburger . . . Pepsipepsipepsi!"

    Garrett Morris, Chico Escuala, "Base-a-ball been a berra berra good to me."

18. These are all famous celebrities and their birth names.

    Orson Bean—Dallas Frederick Burrows

    Jack Benny—Benjamin Kubelsky

    Whoopi Goldberg—Caryn Elaine Johnson

    Cary Grant—Archibald Alexander Leach

    Twiggy—Leslie Hornby

19. These are the characters in the board game Clue.

    Col. Mustard

    Miss Scarlet

    Mr. Green

    Professor Plum

    Mrs. Peacock

20. These are TV sitcom husbands and wives.

    Herman and Lily (*The Munsters*)

    Mike and Carol (*The Brady Bunch*)

    Archie and Edith (*All in the Family*)

    Ray and Debra (*Everybody Loves Raymond*)

    Paul and Jamie (*Mad About You*)

    George and Louise (*The Jeffersons*)

21. These are lead singers and their bands.

Mick Jagger—The Rolling Stones

Gordon Sumner (Sting)—The Police

Paul Hewson (Bono)—U2

David Lee Roth—Van Halen

Steven Tyler—Aerosmith

22. These are famous front-singers and their backup singers.

Gladys Knight and the Pips

Smokey Robinson and the Miracles

Diana Ross and the Supremes

Frankie Lymon and the Teenagers

Little Caesar and the Romans

23. These are famous front-singers and their backup bands.

KC and the Sunshine Band

Bob Marley and the Wailers

Bruce Hornsby and the Range

Bruce Springsteen and the E Street Band

Paul Revere and the Raiders

24. These are famous lead singers and their bands.

> Roger Daltrey—The Who
> Paul Stanley—KISS
> Freddie Mercury—Queen
> Jerry Garcia—The Grateful Dead

25. These are rock stars and their real names.

> Bono—Paul Hewson
> Sting—Gordon Sumner
> Elton—Reginald Kenneth Dwight
> Ringo—Richard Starkey
> Sonny—Salvatore Phillip Bono
> Meat Loaf—Marvin Lee Aday

26. These are celebrities and their birth names.

> Woody Allen—Allen Stewart Konigsberg
> Alan Alda—Alphonso Joseph D'Abruzzo
> Bea Arthur—Bernice Frankel
> Fred Astaire—Frederick Austerlitz
> Lauren Bacall—Betty Joan Perske

27. These are old country names and the names we know
them by now.

      Siam—Thailand

      Formosa—Taiwan

      Ceylon—Sri Lanka

      Hellas—Greece

      Persia—Iran

      Mesopotamia—Iraq

28. Basketball players and the teams they played for.

      Julius Erving—Philadelphia 76ers

      Kareem Abdul-Jabbar—Los Angeles Lakers

      Larry Bird—Boston Celtics

      Michael Jordan—Chicago Bulls

      Patrick Ewing—New York Knicks

      Hakeem Olajuwon—Houston Rockets

      John Stockton—Utah Jazz

29. These are varieties of fruits.

      Valencia orange

      Rainier cherry

      Fuji apple

      Bosc pear

      Concord grape

30. These are states and the fruits they are known for.

Georgia—peach

Maine—blueberry

Florida—orange

California—raisin

Washington—apple

Massachusetts—cranberry

Hawaii—pineapple

31. These are species of animals.

stickleback—fish

flying fox—bat

blue-footed booby—bird

Manx—cat

muntjac—deer

whippet—dog

32. These are colors.

azure—blue

magenta—pink

vermilion—red

sienna—brown

olive—green

33. These are common phrases containing elements.

  carbon (C) copy

  gold (Au) digger

  iron (Fe) fist

  silver (Ag) lining

  lead (Pb) weight

  neon (Ne) sign

34. These are anatomical names and common names of body parts.

  patella—kneecap

  larynx—voice box

  scapula—shoulder blade

  clavicle—collarbone

  trachea—windpipe

35. These are state mottoes.

  Eureka—California

  Live Free or Die—New Hampshire

  Industry—Utah

  Forward—Wisconsin

  Equal Rights—Wyoming

36. These are painting titles and the artists who made them.

Starry Night—Vincent van Gogh

My Mother—James McNeill Whistler

American Gothic—Grant Wood

Water Lilies—Claude Monet

Mother and Child—Mary Cassatt

Sunlight on the Coast—Winslow Homer

37. These are wine grapes and their countries of origin.

Barbera—Italy

Merlot—France

Zinfandel—Croatia

Concord—America

Riesling—Germany

FIND THE MISFIT ANSWERS
pages 248–269

1. Chocolate-chip cookie recipe
MISFITS: olive oil and raisins

2. Chinese zodiac animals
MISFITS: donkey and bear

3. Canadian provinces—Currently there are ten
provinces and three territories (Northwest
Territories, Nunavut, and Yukon)
MISFITS: Windsor (Ontario) and Victoria (BC)

4. Weapons in the board game Clue.
MISFITS: ice pick and chainsaw

5. Jazz trumpet players
MISFITS: Charlie Parker played sax and Glenn Miller
played trombone

6. Pieces in the board game Monopoly
MISFITS: mouse and cow

7. U.S. presidents
MISFITS: Franklin and Hamilton

8. State capitals
MISFITS: New York (should be Albany) and Albuquerque
(should be Santa Fe)

9. Four Gospels of the bible
MISFITS: Paul and George

10. Shakespearean plays

    MISFITS: *Canterbury Tales* (Chaucer) and *A Tale of Two Cities* (Dickens)

11. Planets

    MISFITS: The Moon (a satellite) and Pluto (considered a dwarf planet since 2007)

12. Greek gods

    MISFITS: Aphrodite and Demeter—both female and therefore godesses

13. Winter Olympics events

    MISFITS: crew and triathlon

14. Crayola crayon colors

    MISFITS: ice and mud

15. African countries

    MISFITS: Paraguay (South America) and Papua New Guinea (South Pacific)

16. Insects (Insects come in all shapes, sizes, colors, and designs, but they all have six jointed legs.)

    MISFITS: spider (arachnid) and centipede (arthropod)

17. Oscar-winning movies for best picture
     MISFITS: *The Color Purple* (nominated for
     eleven awards and won zero) and *Star Wars*
     (won six awards but not best picture)

18. Holidays on the U.S. calendar
     June 14, Flag Day; March 17, St. Patrick's Day;
     October 31, Halloween; October 12, Columbus Day;
     October 24, United Nations Day; April 22, Earth Day;
     February 2, Groundhog Day; November 11,
     Veterans Day.
     MISFITS: January 14 and September 7

19. Birds representing North American sports teams
     Oriole (Baltimore baseball),
     Cardinal (St. Louis baseball),
     Blue jay (Toronto baseball),
     Eagle (Philadelphia football),
     Hawk (Atlanta basketball),
     Falcon (Atlanta football),
     Raven (Baltimore football),
     Penguin (Pittsburgh ice hockey)
     MISFITS: heron and seagull

20. U.S. statesmen appearing on U.S. money

Abraham Lincoln ($5 bill),

George Washington ($1 bill),

Benjamin Franklin ($100 bill),

Ulysses S. Grant ($50 bill),

Andrew Jackson ($20 bill),

William McKinley ($500 bill),

Grover Cleveland ($1,000 bill)

MISFITS: Theodore Roosevelt and John Adams

21. Reed instruments

MISFITS: harp (string) and trombone (brass)

22. Roman mythological figures

MISFITS: Zeus and Athena, who are Greek mythological figures

23. Cocktails

MISFITS: Cha Cha Cha and Flight to Mars

24. Cars

Ford Bronco, Jeep Wrangler, Dodge Dakota,
GMC Yukon, Nissan Frontier, Toyota Tundra,
Ford Explorer

MISFITS: Gold Rush and Cowboy

25. Rainforest animals

MISFITS: lion and porcupine

MEMORY BOX #6 ANSWERS
pages 270–273

1. four; **2.** black (three); **3.** cattle; **4.** four; **5.** two; **6.** to the left; **7.** up; **8.** one; **9.** day; **10.** a coyote and a bird

CHAPTER SEVEN
THAT'S LOGICAL

BRAIN MELTERS ANSWERS
pages 277–303

1. There were 162 clams to begin with.
Chip ate 54, leaving 108 clams.
Al ate 36, leaving 72.
And Joe ate 24, leaving 48 clams—which they
divided by three in equal portions of 16.

2. She took the sign and pointed Cortona in the direction from which she had just come. That made the sign correct, and she was able to go in the right direction to Perugia.

3. After a delicious lunch doused in **chile**s from Raj, **a pan**-Asian spot on the avenue, Vi**c had** pains in his chest, **chin, a**nd throat that worried him. He decided **to go** to the emergency room. "**Can a da**sh of hot sauce cause this amount of pain?" he screamed. "Watch your an**ger, man**! **Y**ou're going to work yourself into a hospital stay if you're not careful."

4. 144 worms: Ralph finds 4 every hour, Rosie finds 5 every hour, and Rhonda eats 3 every hour. That makes 6 worms left over each hour. 6 worms x 24 hours = 144 worms left at the end of the day.

5. #1—Keith, age 20
   #2—Kai, age 14
   #3—Leo, age 17
   #4—Lynn, age 22

6. Brawl: Each of the other words remains a real word if you take off the first letter.

7. Collie: For each row find the letter that comes next in the alphabet and then read those letters from the top down.

8.
   1. Sam Splash
   2. Laneline Lena
   3. Goggles McCormick
   4. Chloe Chlorine
   5. Peyton Poule
   6. Wanda Wader
   7. J. B. Jammer
   8. Pat Paddler
   9. Buck Brick
   10. Trenton Trout

9. Inside a roll of toilet paper.

10. Pete's petri dish was half full at 11:59. The next minute there were twice as many bacteria there (so it was full at 12:00).

11. Ned and Ina won with 11 points.

12. | Name | Chose |
|---|---|
| Dinah | Joan Baez |
| Lena | Patti Smith |
| Kathy | Donny Osmond |
| Mary | Dolly Parton |
| Liz | Led Zeppelin |
| George | ABBA |

13. 12

14. | # | Name | Song |
|---|---|---|
| 1 | Ida | "Stayin' Alive" |
| 2 | Eunice | "Freebird" |
| 3 | Madge | "You Really Got Me" |
| 4 | Vera | "I Will Survive" |

15. 44 candles

$$4 (x + 4) + 5 (x + 5) = 10 x$$
$$x = (4 \times 4) + (5 \times 5) = 41$$
$$41 + 3 = 44$$

16. 1,000: one thousand.

17.

Woman	Color	Guy
Lulu Flaymon	Pink	Brock
Frieda Bellabella	Red	Ewan
Hortense Hubbahubba	Blue	Dylan

18. 10 cockroaches, 5 cats, and 35 parakeets

19. 23,475

20. 8 scarves

21. A river

22. She was the lighthouse keeper.

23. Four: Dessert 1–Plate 1; Dessert 1–Plate 2; Dessert 2–Plate 1; Dessert 2–Plate 2.

24. 6 choices: Papaya–Plate 1, Mango–Plate 2; Papaya–Plate 1, Mango–Plate 3; Mango–Plate 1, Papaya–Plate 2; Mango–Plate 1, Papaya–Plate 3; Papaya–Plate 2, Mango–Plate 3; Mango–Plate 2, Papaya–Plate 3.

25. September. The equation is $(((366 + 11) \div 13) + 31 + 3) \div 7 = 9$.

PHONING IT IN ANSWERS

pages 304–305

1. They never took baths!
2. Reptiles!
3. She was a plant eater!
4. It's dinosore!
5. Plenty of room!

BEHIND THE EIGHT BALL ANSWERS

pages 306–307

IF A=S AND S=K, THEN:

A=S	**H**=Z	**O**=G	**V**=N
B=T	**I**=A	**P**=H	**W**=O
C=U	**J**=B	**Q**=I	**X**=P
D=V	**K**=C	**R**=J	**Y**=Q
E=W	**L**=D	**S**=K	**Z**=R
F=X	**M**=E	**T**=L	
G=Y	**N**=F	**U**=M	

1. Her horoscope said:
   Pay attention to the signs.

2. Her fortune cookie said:
   Money will come your way today.

3. A psychic stopped her on the street and said:
   You will be rich!

4. The Ouiji Board said:
   Today is your lucky day.

5. And her clairvoyant Grandson said:
   Buy a lottery ticket!

MORSE CODE ANSWERS
pages 308–310

1. Rash decisions
2. There was a big cover up.
3. He made a clean getaway
4. He got mugged
5. Someone squealed

BUSTED! ANSWERS

pages 311–313

1. Beethoven
2. Brahms
3. Tchaikovsky
4. Chopin
5. Schubert

6. Copland
7. Liszt
8. Prokofiev
9. Haydn
10. Bach

MEMORY BOX #7 ANSWERS

pages 314–317

1. five; 2. Patricia; 3. cat; 4. above; 5. snake;
6. Cindy; 7. Amy; 8. Uncle Ned; 9. Patricia and
Mama Lena; 10. singing